MIRACLE OF THE SONG

MIRACLE of the SONG

By NORMA R. YOUNGBERG

Illustrated by Harold Munson

TEACH Services, Inc.
Ringgold, GA

**PRINTED IN
THE UNITED STATES OF AMERICA**

World rights reserved. This book or any portion thereof may not be copied or reproduced in any form or manner whatever, except as provided by law, without the written permission of the publisher, except by a reviewer who may quote brief passages in a review.

The author assumes full responsibility for the accuracy of all facts and quotations as cited in this book.

Facsimile Reproduction

As this book played a formative role in the development of Christian thought and the publisher feels that this book, with its candor and depth, still holds significance for the church today. Therefore the publisher has chosen to reproduce this historical classic from an original copy. Frequent variations in the quality of the print are unavoidable due to the condition of the original. Thus the print may look darker or lighter or appear to be missing detail, more in some places than in others.

Copyright © 2005 TEACH Services, Inc.
ISBN-13: 978-1-4796-0447-0
Library of Congress Control Number: 00-109023

Published by
TEACH Services, Inc.
www.TEACHServices.com

For Donnie and Linda

Contents

1. THE FIGHT 9
2. INTO THE MOUNTAIN . . . 24
3. THE SONG OF TOGOP . . . 42
4. THE NEW WITCHCRAFT . . . 59
5. THE ELUSIVE DEVIL . . . 75
6. ALL IS NOT ENOUGH . . . 93
7. THE CURSE OF TEEPOO . . . 110
8. THE FALLEN SPARROW . . . 126
9. STRONG MEDICINE 140
10. ROASTED PADI 151
11. SOME SURPRISES 173

1. The Fight

"Not fair! Not fair!" Damin called loudly, and spread his hands in a warning gesture over the two fighting cocks. The two boys kneeling on the ground beside the angry birds grabbed them and stood up, eying each other fiercely. The cocks struggled and twisted in a vain effort to get at each other.

"It is not fair for one bird to have knives and the other one none." Damin looked at Kasar, the owner of the white cock, with anger in his brown eyes.

"It is fair enough," mumbled Kasar, looking at the ground and digging his toe deeper and deeper into the nest of an ant lion. "If I want my cock to fight with knives, it is fair enough." He stared de-

10 MIRACLE OF THE SONG

fiantly at Damin and at Pala, Damin's younger brother, who held his black cock in his arms.

"Come now, Kasar, untie the knives from that cock's legs and we will have a fair fight. You know what is right as well as we do." Damin took the sullen youngster by the shoulder. "You know the best cock should win, not because of concealed knives, but because he is a clever fighter."

Kasar still dug his toe into the ant lion's hole and

THE FIGHT 11

pouted. Pala set the black cock on the ground and began teasing him with his finger, so that his urge to fight should not cool off while Kasar made up his mind. Damin waited patiently. He knew that Kasar loved a cockfight more than any other sport. He knew that Kasar was afraid that his white cock would be beaten, for Pala's black cock was known as the keenest fighter among all the village fowls. So Kasar had concealed a tiny sharp knife among

the feathers on each of the white cock's legs, hoping they would not be noticed. But Damin's eyes were sharp.

"Oh, well, I will take them out." Kasar slowly and reluctantly untied the knives and twisted them into his loincloth. Then he knelt to place his cock beside Pala's. The two cocks circled around each other with graceful archings of their necks and flirtings of their long tails. They sparred with each other in a trial of strength. Then, as courage mounted and the fighting spirit within them swelled, they flew at each other and began a terrible battle. The boys shouted encouragement and approval.

Villagers gathered around and watched with eager interest. Not much could be seen but a whirl of feathers and dust, but it was possible to see that the black was more often on top than the white. Finally the two boys grabbed the mass of whirling feathers, and each one held his cock in his arms to give him a rest and a careful examination for possible wounds.

After a few minutes the cocks were placed on

the ground again and the fight began once more. At last the white cock lay on the ground, completely winded. The black one, knowing himself the victor, strutted and crowed in a loud voice.

"The black won! The black won!" screamed the crowd.

"How much will you take for your cock, boy?"

Pala looked up into the face of Teepoo, the village medicine man, who was Kasar's father and an important man in Lansat Village. "Oh, I will not sell him." Pala was in a flutter of excitement. "I have him well trained now. I know how good he is." His face glowed with pride, and he failed to see the expression on the witch doctor's face, but Damin saw it and understood that Teepoo had been offended.

"I almost think it would have been best for you to sell your cock to Teepoo," Damin said to his brother as they walked home.

"No, I will not sell him." Pala looked down at the black cock nestled in the curve of his arm. "I raised him from a little chicken and I do not have to sell him just because Teepoo wants him. He wants to give him to Kasar to make me sorry and ashamed." Pala looked so troubled that Damin laughed at him and tickled the black cock's comb and wattle. "All right, all right. But it is not good to offend Teepoo. He might make bad medicine against us."

"I am not afraid of Teepoo's medicine," Pala boasted.

"That is easy to say, young fellow, but some day it might be different. Some day you might be in trouble and only Teepoo could help you out of it. Remember that."

The two boys reached the hut at the edge of the village, where they lived with their mother, Teejah. Their father had died of fever when Pala was just a baby. Times had been hard, but now the boys were growing up and could help with planting and caring for the rice fields. Rice is the chief food on the island of Borneo, and Teejah was glad that now the boys could help her with the work of growing it.

Damin was fourteen and Pala ten years old. They had built a neat little thatched hut. The

THE FIGHT

walls were made of palm leaves folded and sewed into rainproof sheets, called *kajang*. The hut was thatched with shingles, called *attap*, made of sago leaves tied so they could be laid on the roof in tiers. Teejah was proud of her home and her two fine sons. No woman in the village worked harder than she did, and the family had planted and harvested and carefully managed their land until they were able to purchase two water buffalo. This made the plowing much easier. Now there were also two young buffalo—a yearling, and a small calf that belonged to Damin and was as dear to his heart as the black cock was to his brother's.

The boys did not go directly into the house, although it was suppertime and they knew the rice in the kettle over the coals was already steamed dry and fluffy. There was good vegetable stew and boiled fish to go with the rice, and they could smell the delicious supper. The two paused where the water buffalo were feeding at the edge of the small clearing.

"This calf grows every day," Pala said.

"Yes, he grows every day, but I can still lift him."

Damin tugged at the sturdy little buffalo calf and finally swung him off the ground.

"My cock is tired." Pala buried his face in the satin feathers. He set the weary bird down and smoothed him and rubbed his slender legs. The cock stood still while Pala opened the little door of a woven basket that hung on the wall of the house, well up under the eaves. Carefully he lifted the black cock and put him inside his basket bedchamber. Then he closed the door and turned to pet the baby water buffalo.

"I will come back and feed the cock after he has rested a little." Pala started up the notched log ladder to the hut just as his mother opened the door and called both boys to come and eat supper.

"Mother, the black cock whipped that white one of Kasar's. Almost everyone came to watch. Teepoo was there and he tried to buy the black cock from Pala." Damin settled himself on the clean mat in the corner of the first room of the hut. Teejah set a plate of steaming rice before him.

"Mother, I do not have to sell my cock, do I?"

Pala received his plate of rice and began eating.

"No, you do not have to sell your cock, son. Perhaps Teepoo will be angry, but he will forget about it in time." Teejah looked fondly at the two boys as they ate a hearty supper. She waited on them until they had finished, then sat down on the mat with her own plate of rice.

"I sunned and dried and stored about half the padi today." Teejah spoke as much to herself as to the boys while she looked at the baskets of unhusked rice she had been working with. "Tomorrow I shall get it all put away. There will be enough for us to eat until the next harvest season and some to sell, so we can buy fish and salt and kerosene and some cloth. I heard queer news today," Teejah went on, looking at Damin to see if he had heard anything strange. But Damin only had news of the cockfight.

"Majang came today from Buluno Village. He says there is a strange witch man come to that village to live." Teejah ate her rice and fish with skillful fingers. "Majang says he is young, but he has powerful medicine."

"I wonder if his medicine is as strong as Teepoo's." Pala lay on the floor, comfortable after his evening meal.

"The medicine is in a black book," Teejah explained. "When the witch man explains to people about the black book, they are changed. They become good and kind."

"I don't believe all that stuff, Mother." Damin's voice was serious. "I hope the new medicine man does not come here. I am afraid of Teepoo and I know he is greedy and mean, but we know him and we know his medicine is powerful."

"Majang says that in a few days he is going up into the mountains to Togop. He will work with the men of that village who will cut down the big jungle for the new season's planting, and he hopes to find a white orchid." Teejah looked at Damin. "He says you may go along, Damin, if you still want to."

Damin knew that his mother was worried about his first venture into the mountains. But he was a man now. Of course he must go. His mind was already off on a fine journey up into the mountains of interior Borneo. There are many wonderful things in the mountains. Wild elephants live there and the fierce *timbado,* a wild cow much bigger than the domestic animals, bigger than the water buffalo—so fierce and vicious that it has been known to lie in wait for hunters and gore them to death with its terrible horns and hoofs.

In the tops of the great trees in the mountain

jungles strange plants grow—parasites that feed on the living trees and lift thick, shiny leaves toward the sunshine. Once or twice a year a spike of flowers unfolds in gorgeous beauty, red, yellow, purple, or white. There in that wonderland of treetops and rain and wind and sunlight, these lovely blossoms flaunt their beauty to the heavens, where no human eye can ever see them and where only the monkeys and birds can enjoy the sight.

Sometimes, when men cut down the trees to make a new field for the mountain rice, and a forest giant shattered to the ground, the strange plants could be found spreading their delicate, waxy bloom among the leaves of the treetop.

The jungle men and women, marveling at the strange beauty of the treetop flowers, carried them home to the village to amuse their children. In the villages white men saw the orchids and bought them, giving salt and red cloth, beads and knives in payment. Purple ones and yellow ones appeared in the markets frequently, but a white orchid was seldom found and so it was a great prize.

THE FIGHT

The high British official in the seaport town had given orders that anyone who found a white orchid should bring it directly to him, and he would pay a fine price for it. Ever since this news had been circulated among the villages, Damin had secretly longed to go to the mountains in quest of the white orchid. He had confided his wish to his mother, and she must have spoken to Majang about it.

Damin wakened from his reverie to find his mother studying his face. "You want to go very much, don't you?" She smiled at him.

"Yes, Mother, I want to go. I will get some rolls of red cloth." His heart beat faster. "I might even get another water buffalo."

Teejah's face lighted with pride, but there was fear in it, too. "Felling the great trees is men's work, Damin. You are strong for your age, but you must be careful."

"Mother, why do the mountain people cut the trees and burn the jungle to plant rice? Why don't they plant it in mud as we do?" Damin was curious.

"It is difficult to make flat fields for growing wet rice on the steep mountainsides. Long ago the mountain people discovered that they could grow one crop of fine rice in the ashes of the burnt-over jungle. They wait until one heavy rain falls on the burnt ground; then the whole village swarms over the place with sharp sticks, making thousands of tiny holes. In each hole they drop a few grains of padi." Teejah knew that Damin had never seen the mountain rice fields so she explained carefully.

Pala went out to feed his black cock. Damin turned the water buffalo out to pasture in the stubble of the rice fields around the village. Teejah carried water from the spring back of the house in joints of bamboo.

"Tomorrow I think you should line the basin at the spring with stones." Teejah spoke to her sons as she lit the coconut-oil lamp and set it on the floor in the middle of the room. "The stream is strong, now that the rains are beginning; the ground has caved in and the place is in disorder. You can make it smooth and neat with the stones."

THE FIGHT

Damin sat in the feeble light with his hands folded, doing nothing. Pala sat close to the light and carved a coconut shell, smoothing and polishing it into a large cup. Teejah wove bamboo strips into a basket. So many baskets were needed about the house—baskets for the chickens, baskets for the rice and the winnowing, baskets to carry the vegetables and the eggs. There was never a time when the weaving of baskets was not a pressing task.

Rain fell early in the night. The boys slept on their mats, one on either side of the small inner room. Damin, waking, listened to the beat of the rain on the thatched roof and felt cold. He pulled his red blanket over him and rolled up in it. He dreamed and his dreams were of cockfights. The white cock seemed very large and his face was the face of Teepoo. Then he looked for the black cock, and it was the new witch man who had come to live in Buluno Village. The two cocks were sparring with each other and the knives were on the legs of the white cock.

2. Into the Mountain

"You know we are really lucky to have a spring like this near our house." It was Damin who spoke. He and Pala had been working for an hour, choosing smooth stones and placing them as a facing in the floor of the basin below the spring.

Their mother came to fill the water bamboos and to encourage the boys in their work. "It might be a good thing to put a fresh bamboo trough in the spring, too," she suggested. Teejah was a neat, careful woman.

After their mother had returned to the hut, both boys rested from their heavy work for a few minutes in the shade of a giant tree whose branches overhung the spring. They had great affection for this old tree. It was because of it that their father had chosen this spot for their home. It was a *buluno* tree, and in the fruit season it bore an abundance of large green fruits as big as grapefruit. These fruits were strongly scented and had a sweet, orange-colored meat like a coarse peach. It was a lucky tree, reported to bring good fortune to those who lived close to it. Damin and Pala leaned against it now and wiped the perspiration from their hot faces.

"Damin, will you go with Majang to hunt the white orchid?" Pala asked.

"I will surely go. I would like nothing better than to find the most beautiful orchid that has ever been brought from the hills."

"What will you do with the reward?" Pala was a great dreamer. His eyes turned now toward the mountains where Kinabalu lifted its majestic head against the blue of the morning sky.

"Plenty of time to think of that when I get it." Damin laughed at his little brother. "I think Majang is coming today to get some of our seed rice." Damin began again to fit the stones to the

curved bowl of the basin beneath the flowing stream of the spring. "We can ask him about that trip into the hills and maybe we can find out more about the young witch doctor who has come to live in his village. I should like to know more about his medicine."

The work at the spring took most of the day. The fowls had to be taken care of and the water

buffalo must be brought back when they wandered too far away. The two boys gave their mother some help in storing the rice. It was nearly evening when Majang appeared, with a bag tightly woven of reed grass. He intended to carry the seed rice home on his shoulder. He was tired from his walk and squatted on the ground beside the cottage to talk with the boys a few minutes.

"Do you think I could go along to look for the white orchid?" Pala squatted down in front of Majang.

"No, you are not big enough," Majang explained. "Felling the big trees is work for strong men, and the journey is hard. Besides, what would your mother do with neither of you boys to help her? No, Pala, wait till you are bigger and stronger. There will still be white orchids in the jungle when you are an old man." Majang laughed and chewed hard on his quid of betel nut.

"When will you go?" Damin asked.

"I should like to start tomorrow," Majang answered. "I want to see this new witch doctor and his medicine making. I must be back before the plowing begins."

"Tell us about the new medicine, Majang. Have you tried any of it?" Both boys were eager to hear.

"I have not tried it." Majang spoke firmly and spat out his betel-nut wad so he could talk better. "That new teacher—he calls himself a teacher, but we know he is a witch doctor—carries a small black book with him wherever he goes. We think the medicine is in the black book. When he sits down to rest he takes out the book and looks in it. Then he appears to be happy." Majang shook his head.

"That sounds like good medicine to me." Damin laughed. "I know of people in Lansat Village who could do with more cheerfulness."

"This young man is different from us. He does not chew the betel nut. He does not smoke or chew tobacco. He will not even taste our liquor. He tells the people not to keep the pigs under their houses. He says they are dirty and smell bad." Majang became more and more excited as he named over all the things that the new teacher disapproved of.

"But why?" Damin had never heard of such things before. "Why won't he chew tobacco and drink liquor?"

"He says there is a great God of Heaven who has sent him to tell us how to make our hearts and bodies clean. He says this God of Heaven wants us to live with him some day, and we must be clean people to live with the God of Heaven. This teaching is in the black book." Majang sighed a troubled sigh and looked up at the calm blue heavens.

"Oh, I don't believe a word of that!" Damin drew some tobacco out of a pouch knotted in the tail of his loincloth and chewed it defiantly. "We have always drunk rice wine and chewed betel nut and tobacco. What can be the harm of that? What pleasure would we have without these things?"

"That's what I say, too." Majang stood up. "But this young man, Rindoo, is full of pleasure. He seems always happy. Also he is very kind. He helps the sick. He thinks about the old folk and he tells stories to the children and plays with them. He tells the people to be kind to each other."

Majang called to Teejah. She opened the door and together they went to the inner room where the rice bin stood, to take out the seed padi that Majang had come to buy. The boys followed them, hoping to hear more about the new teacher in Buluno Village, but Majang talked only about the trip into the mountains and said that he would come for Damin early in the morning.

"Teepoo is going to be very angry about this new witch doctor." Damin spoke thoughtfully to his brother when they were alone again. "The people from Buluno Village have always called Teepoo in case of sickness and to show them the proper times to plant rice and get married. He has always made medicine for them and charms for their children."

"Maybe the new teacher might come over here some time," Pala suggested. "That would really make Teepoo angry." Pala laughed as though it would not bother him at all to see Teepoo angry.

"Come on, you fellows. We have time for a fight before it gets too dark." Both boys turned to find Kasar holding his white cock in his arms. The sun was just going down and the twilight is short in Borneo. Damin was surprised. It is not usual to have a cockfight except in broad daylight.

"Turn that cock around, Kasar." Damin pulled the smaller boy toward him, but Kasar jerked away.

"Just as I thought! You hoped no one would see those knives on your cock's legs in the dark." Damin was angry. "Go home. Cheat somebody else, but don't try your tricks on us."

Both boys stood watching Kasar shuffle down through the huts toward his father's house. "He is going to kill your black cock by his tricks or he is going to work out some scheme so you will have to let him have your cock," Damin warned his brother. "Come, I know what we must do."

Damin struck off into the grass and brush surrounding the village. Water-buffalo trails wound through it and crisscrossed everywhere. The two boys hurried along until they came to the other end of the village. It was dusk now. They crept under the witch doctor's house, avoiding the pigs that were kept there, hiding themselves among the baskets and other rubbish that littered the space. The floor of the house was of split bamboo and it was easy to hear conversation, especially when the voices were loud and angry as they were tonight.

"I do not think you are a good witch doctor,"

Kasar was saying to his father. "If you were you would get the black cock for me. Everyone in the village is laughing at me and you know it. Your medicine is no good at all!"

"Young fool," his father exclaimed. "Have patience. I have already promised you that I will get the black cock for you. Some things take time. You will have to learn to wait. Oh, yes, I know you have been laughed at. What does that matter when you know you are going to win what you want and laugh back?" Teepoo talked louder and louder. Kasar was excited and angry. He would not be soothed.

Damin and Pala had heard enough. They knew that Teepoo would use all the witchcraft at his command to satisfy the whim of his only son. With quiet steps they picked their way out of the rubbish. The pigs were disturbed and grunted their disapproval, but the argument between the witch doctor and his son was so loud and furious that no attention was paid to the pigs. The boys walked back through the village in the early darkness.

"Oh, where have you been?" exclaimed Teejah. "I have looked everywhere for you."

"We just walked down through the village." Damin came up the ladder into the house. Both boys washed their feet and went into the inner room.

Teejah settled herself on her mat and took up her work of sewing palm leaves into wide sheets of rectangular shape. These sheets of *kajang* would be useful for many things. They were excellent covering for walls, being waterproof. They could also be used for covering things so they might be kept dry during the rains. Teejah folded the sheets in a neat pile beside the rice bin.

The boys did not tell their mother of the conversation overheard under Teepoo's house. It would be a dangerous thing for anyone to know that they had spied on the house of the witch doctor. It might be their mother would disapprove. She was certain to be unhappy about it. Better say nothing.

Pala slept soundly in spite of his worry over the

black cock, but Damin tossed on his mat. His mind was full of the journey to the hills and the white orchid. He got up twice to peer out through the small window of the hut. Of course there was nothing outside the window, nothing but the rainy night and the waving bamboo and the water buffalo grazing along the edge of the rice field.

So at last the great morning came, with sunshine after the rain. As Majang and Damin picked their way through the wet grass of the narrow path along the border of the rice fields, Damin was happy. Ahead and above them towered the hills and beyond them the high mountains. Somewhere on that enchanted upland was the white orchid, the prize that he hoped to win.

"Perhaps the mountain people will not allow us to take the white orchid if we find it." Damin was worried. "I wonder if they know how much the white man values the flower."

Majang set the *bohongan* he was carrying down in the path and Damin loosened the head strap of his own *bohongan* and knelt with it, withdrawing his arms from the straps.

"The mountain people are simple." Majang rubbed his forehead. "They don't know what the plants are worth. They value them only by the taste. If they are good to eat with the rice, then they boil and eat them. As for flowers being of value to look at—faugh! That would sound like nonsense to them."

The travelers leaned against their *bohongans*. These cup-shaped containers made of bark are about three feet high and are fitted with a tight lid. There are two heavy loops of bark at each side for the arms to pass through and another longer loop, which is adjusted to cross the forehead, so that the burden is carried and balanced with one's whole body. This is important on the steep hills.

Majang pulled the lid off his *bohongan*, took out a small box, and rolled himself a wad of betel nut. Damin followed his example. The two looked back down the path they had traveled, and chewed and spat and rested.

"We cross a stream before we start climbing, don't we?" Damin was beginning to feel thirsty.

"Yonder, just where those trees cluster at the

foot of the hill." Majang pointed far up the trail.

After resting a few minutes they knelt and slipped their arms through the carrying loops of their *bohongans,* adjusted the head straps, and jogged along the trail which still led through the rice fields across the level land. It was midmorning when they reached the stream. They rested the *bohongans* against the large rocks and drank deeply, then stood leaning against them with their tired feet in the cool, flowing water. The leafy

foliage of the overhanging branches brushed their faces as they enjoyed the welcome shade and the coolness of the stream.

"Look out! Look out!" Majang screamed.

Damin had caught a flicker of movement among the green leaves. He ducked his head, bending forward quickly. A dull thump against the lid of the bark *bohongan* was followed by a much louder thud as Majang brought a stout stick down on the green snake.

"Ayoh! Ayoh!" Majang gasped with excitement as he disentangled the reptile from the thick foliage and laid him, still writhing, on the rocks. "Lucky for you, you are quick. Otherwise—well, you would never see the mountains and the white orchid."

"He was aiming for my head, wasn't he?" Damin shuddered as he looked at the long green snake lying broken on the rock before him. It was a hamadryad, a deadly reptile that lives in the leafy branches of the Borneo jungle.

"We must go." Majang hurried to adjust his

burden and move on. "These snakes always go two and two. There is another somewhere among these leaves."

"Do you think we should go on?" Damin wet his dry lips. "Is it not an evil omen?"

"The snake was behind us, Damin, so we cannot turn back."

In spite of his narrow escape and his fright, Damin moved with quick, sure strides and they were soon across the stream and beginning the ascent of the first long hill. Monkeys called with shrill chatter from the jungle about them. Bright butterflies darted before them along the path wherever they emerged into the sunshine. The path was slick from the rain that fell every night. It required skill to balance the *bohongans* and scramble up the steep and rugged way. The bark thongs of the *bohongans* swung to the shifting weight with loud, creaking noises, the music of the trail.

3. The Song of Togop

About midday the two came out into an old rice field on the steep side of a hill. Here they put down their burdens and sat in the shade of an abandoned hut. They could look out over the valley below and the ocean, which stretched away to the horizon, a sheet of cobalt blue beneath a sapphire sky. Over all shimmered the intense sunshine, damp and hot.

"Are we halfway there?" Damin turned to look at the path that stretched away, up and around the hill.

"I think we are halfway there," Majang encouraged the boy. "The last part of the way is no harder than what we have already passed."

At sundown the two came abruptly to the top

of a wooded mountain. Below them on the far side stretched the clearing where the village of Togop stood, its stilted huts sprawled over the mountainside. A new one, larger than the rest, stood at the upper edge of the clearing. Dogs and pigs swarmed under the huts and among them. Water buffalo fed at the outskirts of the village.

"Yonder is the house of my friend, Lootoo, where we will stay." Majang led the way to a thatched hut near the center of the cluster of houses.

Their coming had been observed, and the villagers came out of their huts to greet the newcomers and ask them about their journey and the purpose of their visit, but Lootoo welcomed them and drew them into his hut. There they loosened the *bohongans* and sat down on the mats to rest. Lootoo called his wife to cook rice for them, and his little boy, Jikkie, entertained them both with bright chatter and shy smiles.

"I will show you the spring," Lootoo offered, for the visitors must refresh themselves after their long journey. At the spring, the two drank with enjoyment and bathed in the cool, flowing water.

"Peace to you, my friends." Both turned to see who had spoken. No one else had been at the spring when they came. It was almost dark, and all the village folk had bathed and carried home the full bamboos before sundown. A young man dressed in white stood beside them. "I am Slamat." The young man spoke in a low, musical voice. "I see you are strangers. I have but lately come to this village too. If you are not too tired, perhaps you will join with us in our singing tonight."

Majang and Damin grunted pleasantly in reply to the stranger's invitation.

The young man had brought a change of clothes with him and he proceeded to bathe and dress himself in fresh white clothing. When he had gathered up his soap and towel, he turned back along the path to the village.

Then Majang spoke. "That fellow looks like Rindoo, the new witch man who has come to our village. Something about his voice and his manner is the same."

THE SONG OF TOGOP

They hurried back to the hut of Lootoo. "Tell us"—Majang grabbed his friend by the shoulder—"tell us, is this stranger who wears white clothes a witch doctor?"

Lootoo laughed. "He is a teacher lately come to our village. I suppose you might call him some kind of a witch doctor. He has good medicine."

"It is the same, the same!" Majang was excited now. "One has come to us in Buluno also," he confided. "He wears the white too and carries a black book, and all the time his voice is full of singing and his face is ready with smiles."

"Do you sing every evening?" Damin asked.

"Yes, and it is a pleasant thing," Lootoo explained. "It makes us glad to come together after our day's work and sing."

Even as the visitors bent over the steaming bowls of rice that Lootoo's wife had prepared, they could hear from the top of the hill the blowing of a buffalo horn and then the sound of singing in a full, clear voice.

Damin hurried to the door of the hut. From the thatched houses below and all around the people were coming, one by one and two by two and family by family. They sang as they came, the same simple song that echoed and re-echoed from the top of the mountain. Damin thought no more of his supper. He followed the others to the teacher's house, where all the streams and trickles of melody from all over the village flowed together into one song.

> *"God will take care of you*
> *Through every day.*
> *O'er all the way*
> *He will take care of you."*

The chorus swelled and lifted as they gathered in the large, open veranda of the new house and sat down on the leaf mats, close together.

Damin had no clear understanding of the words of the song, although they were words of his own language. But as the song was repeated, he found himself joining in and singing with the others.

Then the young teacher spoke to the listening people. "Think about these words we are singing," he said. "They mean that the God of Heaven loves all men. Try to take this into your hearts. You are not alone. The God of Heaven is with you always."

Two other songs were sung. They were not so well known as the first, but with the guidance of the young teacher they were not difficult, and both were repeated many times. After an hour of singing the people departed for their huts, still singing as they went, and the song floated here and there throughout the village until the last straggler had entered his own door. Then the friendly dark closed down.

Damin lay on his mat rolled up in his red blanket. He dozed and started in his sleep. He saw the green snake twisting toward him out of the green leaves. Then a wave of song broke over him.

> *"God will take care of you*
> *Through every day.*
> *O'er all the way*
> *He will take care of you."*

Finally he fell asleep and did not waken until Majang shook him in the early morning. "Come, Damin, we are going now." The villagers were departing for their day's work on the other slope of the mountain.

"They have just started to cut the big trees," Majang explained to Damin as they followed the men along the narrow path, newly cut through the tall grass and brush.

Arrived at the spot, the men—about twenty of them—fell to cutting and clearing. Their only tool for such work was a heavy knife, so all the trees had to be felled by hacking them bit by bit. The small trees and brush had already been cut down over the whole area. Majang and Damin had brought along their heavy jungle knives, and they bent their backs to the hard work of felling the great trees along with the men of Togop Village.

"Come, let us eat and rest," Lootoo urged them. He took out a basket of rice cakes. Each rice cake had been wrapped in an individual basket of leaves and boiled in coconut milk. Nothing could have been more delicious after a morning of strenuous labor.

"Have you tried the new witch man's medicine?" Damin asked Lootoo, as the three sat on the trunk of a felled tree enjoying the rice cakes.

"Only the singing." Lootoo smiled. "The singing makes gladness in the heart, so I think it is good medicine."

"You remember I told you that one of these teachers has come to our village." Majang bent forward with a troubled look on his face. "Why do they come, Lootoo? Why do they come?"

"Slamat says he came because the God of Heaven sent him to bring us good news and great joy." Lootoo talked as if he was favorable to the teacher.

"Has he told you what the good news is?" Majang was skeptical. "I think these young men are planning to change our customs and destroy our pleasures. Rindoo, the new witch doctor in my village, says we should not use betel nut or tobacco or liquor. If these are taken from us, what pleasures will we have left?" Majang scowled and searched Lootoo's face.

"I don't know exactly what the good news is except that the teacher says the God of Heaven is kind. He thinks this God is more powerful than our spirits." Lootoo scratched his head. "Slamat has only been here one moon of days and most of that time he has been building his house. We helped him with the house, or it would still be unfinished."

The simple meal was soon eaten. The other villagers were hard at work again, so the three friends joined them and the talk about the new teacher ceased. But over and over the melody of the song came back to Damin with part of the words: "God will take care of you." Who was this God who would promise to take care of just anyone? How could he do it? What sort of being was he? Damin thought about it all day.

Several of the big trees were felled that day, and Majang hurried to examine them for orchid plants, but there were none. Late in the afternoon

THE SONG OF TOGOP

the tired villagers sheathed their knives and climbed the trail over the crest of the mountain to their homes.

Back in the village everyone went to the spring to bathe and refresh themselves. Hot rice was steaming over the coals and Damin discovered that felling jungle trees gives one an enormous appetite. In spite of his weariness and hunger and disappointment over finding no orchids, Damin's heart was unaccountably light as he sat with his plate of rice on the floor of Lootoo's hut. His ears were listening. Eager excitement filled his mind. Would it come again tonight? Would it be the same?

Darkness had fallen. The coconut-oil lamp had been lighted. Yes, there it was—the blowing of the buffalo horn and the clear, strong voice of the young teacher raised in song. Then the miracle was repeated. The singing people left their huts and climbed the steep mountainside to the teacher's house. Stronger and stronger, the music swelled and flowed together until a mighty chorus rang out over the dark valley and all the people were settled on their mats in Slamat's house.

Damin responded at the first summons of the horn and went up, singing with the others, to join the chorus on the new teacher's veranda. He looked for Majang to come, but Majang did not come. Lootoo and his wife and little Jikkie came among the first.

The enchanted hour was soon over, and as before the teacher spoke to the people about the God of Heaven. Then they dispersed, singing as they went, until all had entered their huts and the silence of night settled down over the mountain village. A sense of peace hung in the night like an actual presence. Damin had felt it the night before, but it was stronger now. The boy lay on his mat, filled with a content he could not explain.

So the days passed. Every morning the men went forth to their work of felling the trees. Every evening the miracle of the song was repeated, and the deep peace of the night.

It was on the evening of the sixth day that the

THE SONG OF TOGOP 53

men who returned to Lootoo's house were met by a wild-eyed, frantic woman. "Where is Jikkie?" screamed Lootoo's wife. "I thought you took him with you. He followed you! My uncle saw him!" The young mother's voice rose to a thin, piercing wail.

The men looked at one another, dumb with astonishment. Then at last they realized that little Jikkie must be lost somewhere on the jungle-covered mountain and that he had been lost all day. Now the sun was going down.

The loud wailing of Jikkie's mother soon brought a crowd of people flocking into the hut to learn the cause of the weeping and screaming. The young teacher, Slamat, came hurrying down as soon as he heard the news.

It was easy to understand. The mother supposed that Jikkie had gone with his father, as he sometimes did. Lootoo thought the child safe at home with his mother. The tiny boy had been left behind on the trail, chasing butterflies perhaps, or gathering wild flowers. Of course the child had lost himself among the branching paths that crossed each other in perplexing confusion.

"Prepare torches!" Slamat took charge of the situation. "We must go out and search for the child at once."

So there was no singing in the village on that night, but there was weeping and grief among the women, who thought of their own little ones and sorrowed for the one that was lost.

All along the jungle trails of Togop Mountain torches flared and voices called loudly into the night, but no answer came back and no trace of the child was found. It had now been many hours since Jikkie had disappeared. No further hope was possible. He must have been carried off and destroyed by some of the wild creatures of the forest.

All the searching parties returned in despair. It was then that the young man, Slamat, spoke. "Do not be discouraged, Lootoo. Let us pray to the God of Heaven, who cares for Jikkie as he cares for all of us. Let us ask God to protect him through this night."

THE SONG OF TOGOP

At this the women only wailed the louder, but Lootoo fixed his sad, dark eyes on Slamat. "Will you ask the God of Heaven to do this thing for me?" Lootoo gazed at the young teacher with his whole heart's desire in his face.

And then the heart of Damin leaped up in wild excitement, for Slamat lifted his face to the heaven of stars and spoke with his hands lifted up, as though expecting them to be filled.

> *"O God of Heaven,*
>   *You who love and pity us all,*
>   *Look on our distress.*
>   *Look on Lootoo and his wife.*
>   *Behold their grief.*
> *Look on the child, Jikkie.*
>   *Keep and protect him from the perils*
>   *of the night.*
>   *Bring back the lost one.*
>   *Our love to you.*
>   *Our thanks to you."*

56   MIRACLE OF THE SONG

When the prayer was ended, the young teacher looked around on them all with affection in his face. "Sleep now, my friends." He hushed them with both upraised hands. "We have asked the

God of Heaven to help us. We must trust him to take care of Jikkie."

"This is strong medicine!" Majang sat down on his sleeping mat and held both hands to his head when they had returned to the hut. "This is strong medicine. I feel its power!"

Lootoo said nothing, but peace was in his face. Damin lay marveling on his mat and felt himself enveloped in a tranquility too deep for words.

Not many hours of darkness were left for sleep. When the sun rose, suddenly a voice of joy was heard. The child, Jikkie, came running down the mountain! "Mama, Papa, where are you?" he called. His father ran to catch him up in his arms. His mother wept again for joy, and all the village people rejoiced. They asked the boy how he had come home and he smiled at them.

"I went far. In the dark time I slept. When day came I was at the top of the mountain. I looked down and saw the village. So I came."

The people stared at each other in amazement, because they knew that no man could wander alone on the mountain in the night and live to tell of it.

And that day Majang decided to go home to Buluno Village, but he would not say why. Damin was surprised and disappointed. They had found three beautiful purple orchids and a yellow one, spotted with brown, which had been carefully potted in coconut fiber. But no white orchid had been found.

Damin knew that Majang was troubled deep in his heart. It was not because Jikkie had come home safe and sound—no one could be sorry for that—but because words spoken to the God of Heaven had such power.

4. The New Witchcraft

THE RETURN JOURNEY was more difficult than the coming had been, because heavy rain fell on that day and sliding down the steep path with the heavy *bohongans* was dangerous. Damin and Majang did not stop to rest and but few words were spoken.

"Strong medicine! Strong medicine!" Majang mumbled once to himself as he swung along the trail.

Damin was sorry to leave Togop Village. He had become interested in the medicine of the young teacher, Slamat. What was it in the songs and the words of the teacher that made such gladness in the heart? From whence came that deep peace of the nights after the singing? And the words that Slamat had spoken to his God about Jikkie. How could one learn to speak such words? And who is this God of Heaven, so great and powerful and yet so near to the need of a little child? Only the spirits had such powers. Was God then a spirit?

So Damin turned these matters over in his mind, but he did not dare to speak of them to Majang. The boy sensed the nature of Majang's fears and was silent.

They reached the stream where the snake had struck at Damin's head. It was swollen from the rain but still passable, and they hurried through. Majang had tied two of the orchids to his *bohongan* and two to Damin's. They looked beautiful and fresh with the drops of rain on the flowers. When they reached Damin's home, it was growing dark and the rain was pelting down in a deluge.

"Stop with us, Majang." Damin laid his hand on his companion's shoulder. "The rice will be ready soon, and after you are rested you may go home."

"No, Damin." Majang rejected the boy's persuasion. "No, I must go on at once."

"Then take these orchids." Damin set his *bohongan* down in the rain in front of his house and began to untie the plants.

"Those two are yours," Majang insisted. "I will see you tomorrow." And he disappeared into the dusk and the rain.

The creak of his swinging *bohongan* drifted back to Damin through the dark. He stood listening until there was no sound but the beating of the rain. Then he threw open the door of the hut, shouting, "Mother! Pala! Where is my supper?"

There was joy in the little house as Teejah blew the fire into bright flame and set fresh rice over it. Pala came and looked at the two strange plants that Damin had brought back. "I thought you went after a white orchid. This one is purple and the other is yellow with brown spots. What is wrong with them? Did they change color in the rain?" Pala teased his brother.

"We did not expect you back so soon." Teejah

studied her son's face. "Did something go wrong?"

"Oh no, Mother, nothing went wrong. But Majang was afraid of the new teacher's medicine and he insisted on coming right home."

Teejah sat down on the mat beside Damin. "Come now, talk slowly. What is all this talk about teachers and medicine? I thought you went to search for the white orchid."

"There is a new teacher in Togop Village like the one who has come to Buluno Village. Every night he calls the village people with singing and they come up the mountain to his house, and they sing very hard and they are glad and they . . ." Damin paused to catch his breath. His mother and Pala listened with eager ears.

"After the singing is over, the teacher tells the people about his God. They all return to their homes, singing as they go. Then great peace comes down over everyone."

"But surely that would not make Majang afraid. He is a good man and brave. He would not be frightened by singing." Teejah's forehead wrinkled up as it always did when she was troubled.

THE NEW WITCHCRAFT 63

"There is more to tell, Mother." Damin went on with enthusiasm. "We stayed in the house of Majang's friend Lootoo. He has a little boy four years old. And yesterday he followed us to the jungle and we didn't know it. His mother thought he was with us until we came back in the evening. Then we all knew the child had followed us and been lost on the mountain. There was much sorrow and crying and the young teacher led us out on the mountain with torches to look for the boy, but we couldn't find him and all of us went back to the village. Then the teacher, standing before us all, lifted up his hands and his face to the God of Heaven, whom he worships, and asked him to protect the little boy from all the dangers of the mountain and the night."

"Oh, Damin," Teejah cried out, "hurry. Tell us, did they find the little one?"

"No, they didn't find him. They went to their sleeping mats, and at sunrise the child came running into the village unhurt."

"Damin!" His mother spoke sharply. "Damin, has this new witchcraft taken your heart?"

Damin looked at his mother in astonishment. "I sang with them. I was there when the child returned. I heard the words. I felt the peace." He pondered in his heart the question his mother had asked him.

"Now I know why Majang hurried to come home." Teejah looked very grave. Then she smiled again, for she was glad that Damin had come back. She looked at the flowers and admired their waxy beauty. She tended the rice while he went to bathe in the rain. She fixed him a good supper and sat by him while he ate. They talked of many things, but they did not mention the new witchcraft again, nor did they speak of the new teachers in Togop Village and Buluno. And Damin did not tell of the green snake that had almost struck him in the head at the stream, for he could not tell this without remembering the words of the song, "God will take care of you." It seemed a certain thing in his mind now that the God of Heaven *had* taken care of him, and the thought could not be gotten rid of, so he did not speak of it.

After Damin had hung the two orchids out on the side of the hut and the family had gone to their sleeping mats, he lay awake in the darkness trying to bring back to his heart the peace of the mountain village. He sang over and over in his mind the songs that Slamat had taught them. Some of them he could remember. And as the words filled his mind, the peace came back and he slept well and woke early, and the rain had stopped.

It was market day and Pala urged him to hurry and take the orchids to the market, because someone might buy them. Even if the price was small, they could have a nice treat.

"I will take only the purple one," Damin decided. "The other one has many flowers yet to open and it will look better when the bloom is full. So I will take only the purple one." The two boys went down the path to the market place.

At the market place they met Majang. He had brought his two purple orchids to market. They decided to display all three of them together, and only a few moments later a Chinese gentleman came along and began bargaining for the three plants. When the sale was completed, the price was better than they had hoped. Majang gave Damin one third of the profits, and he felt quite rich. The boys thought of what their mother might like and they wandered all over the market selecting dried fish, Chinese pickled mustard, and as many other good things to eat as they could afford. They even bought three tins of American sardines in tomato sauce as a special treat.

Laden with all this wealth, they came home late in the afternoon and surprised their mother. Teejah was in a flutter of excitement over all this unexpected food.

"We shall have a wonderful supper tonight," Pala told Damin as they bathed at the spring.

After supper Damin played with his baby water buffalo, and the warm familiar feeling of home enfolded him again. The happenings at Togop seemed misty and far away.

The next morning both boys worked hard in the

hot sun cutting sago leaves and stacking them. At noon they sat down to rest on the shady side of the hut, just beneath the basket where Pala kept his black cock. The cock kept sticking his head out through the holes in the loosely woven basket and looking down at the two boys in a friendly way.

Pala lay sprawled on the grass. Damin sat cross-legged, leaning against one of the poles on which the hut was supported. He held his head in his hands for a while, then a shaking seized him and

he began to tremble all over. Soon his teeth chattered and clinked together. Pala spoke to him. He did not answer. His eyes had a wild, bloodshot look.

"Mother! Mother!" Pala scrambled up the ladder into the hut. "Damin has the fever!"

Teejah hurried down to her son. She helped him to his feet and half dragged him up the ladder into the hut and to his sleeping mat. She wrapped the red blanket around him and sat stroking his head with her hands, her heart full of fear. This was nothing new or strange. The fever often struck suddenly. Her husband had been taken just so and he had never recovered.

All through the afternoon she sat by Damin's side, watching him anxiously. "Go to sleep, Pala," she said at last. "There is nothing you can do for Damin. I will stay with him. You have already taken care of the animals, and I filled the bamboos."

The rain began, beating on the roof with a mournful patter. Teejah set the coconut-oil lamp in the corner of the room, where the feeble light would not shine in the boy's face. She watched him until the shaking stopped and his hands and face and body grew hot with fever.

"Water, water!" Damin cried again and again through the night. As Teejah lifted his head so that he could drink from the coconut cup, she felt how hot he was. Toward morning the fever left and the boy broke into an exhausting sweat, then sank into such a limp and listless weariness that he lay on his mat all day with scarcely a word or a movement. Teejah brought him food, but he ate little. Pala did all the chores. The neighbors came in to look at the sick boy and to offer advice about his care. Teejah sat by Damin's side all that night.

At dawn she went to the spring to bathe and to fill the empty bamboos. She paused for a moment near the great tree, thinking, as she often did, of her husband, who had loved it. Then she remembered how he had fallen ill with the fever, just as Damin had done, and fear swept over her as she hastened back to the sick boy.

The following day at noon Damin was seized again with a severe chill, even more terrible than the first one. When the fever came on, he became delirious and talked wildly of the white orchid and Teepoo and mumbled the songs he had learned from the teacher in Togop Village. He tried to get up from his mat and walk, but Teejah and Pala prevented him. His cries for water rang out through all the third night.

"Teejah, you should build a fire on his chest." One of the neighbor women had come in to look at Damin on the fourth day of his illness. The fever had again left him weak and stupid. "The Chinese always build a fire on a sick person's chest. It is a sure way to burn the devils out."

"I'm not clever at such things," Teejah replied through tight lips.

"I'll help you," offered the neighbor.

The two of them managed to build a tiny fire right at the base of Damin's breast bone. As it scorched his tender flesh, he stirred and threw his arms around in pain.

"See, the devil is leaving," exclaimed the neighbor. "It always works."

THE NEW WITCHCRAFT

When the visitor had gone and the fire had been removed, Damin sank back into the apathy that had oppressed him all day, but now he held one hand over the burned spot and sometimes cried out or moaned a little when he dropped off to sleep.

Every night the rain fell. Every night Teejah kept watch over Damin. A dark cloud hung over the little hut, a cloud so dark it could be felt. Pala felt it. He had no joy in anything. The black cock clamored in vain for attention. Pala fed him, but that was all.

It was on the fifth day, when the onset of chills was still more violent, that Majang appeared. He had come to the village on some errand and, hearing of Damin's illness, had come to offer his advice. "Rindoo, the new teacher in Buluno Village, might be able to make medicine for Damin," he suggested, looking down with compassion on the boy, whose body was shaken with such violence that he seemed to be in a convulsion. "He has helped some in our village who were taken with such fevers."

72   MIRACLE OF THE SONG

"Oh, Majang, I am afraid of that teaching." Teejah was weeping. "Do you think Teepoo could do anything?"

"I am afraid of the new witchcraft too," Majang admitted, "but I can see that it is powerful medicine." He scuffed his bare toes along the split bamboo of the floor. "I suppose Teepoo should be able to help. You have quite a few chickens. Perhaps you have some choice rolls of cloth in your

chest there." He indicated the wooden chest that always stood by Teejah's sleeping mat. "You have the water buffalo. It should be possible for you to have a good lot of medicine made for Damin." Majang tried to sound hopeful. "You know, it is strange." He stroked his chin reflectively. "That teacher, Rindoo, won't accept any chickens, or cloth, or anything when he makes the medicine."

"Then it surely cannot be good." Teejah had made up her mind. "I think you should go over and call Teepoo. Tell him how sick Damin is and ask him to come over and see if his charms will help." She sat quietly for a moment. "Oh, yes, Majang. Tell him I will be glad to pay him what he requires for his services."

Pala and his mother waited beside Damin in the fading light. He was burning with fever now and the delirium was on him. It took all their attention to care for him. When he was finally quieted, the night was far gone. Teepoo had not come. Majang had not returned. In the morning both Teejah and Pala were so weary they could scarcely stand, but Pala forced himself to care for the chickens and even carried water from the spring, although that was woman's work and he could never have been persuaded to do it under other circumstances.

"Pala, perhaps Majang did not find Teepoo," Teejah whispered to her youngest son. "You had better run and ask him to come quickly."

"Mother, Teepoo is angry with me because of the cockfight. You remember he wanted to buy my cock and I would not sell it to him."

"No, no, Pala. The witch doctor would not take up a child's quarrel like that. Run and tell him to come quickly." Teejah rubbed Damin's cold, wet hands. The fever had gone and left him like one dead.

5. The Elusive Devil

WHEN PALA RETURNED from his errand to Teepoo, his face looked so pale and pinched that his mother caught his hand and drew him down on the mat beside her. "What is wrong, Pala? Don't you feel well?"

Pala's teeth began to chatter, although it was midmorning and the sun was warm. "I—I—think—I am getting the sickness too." He shuddered. Teejah made him lie down on the mat at the other side of the small room. When Teepoo came at noon he found her there, sitting with bowed head between the two sick boys.

Damin was now so weak that chills and fever swept over him like waves of the sea over a stranded boat. There was little response of any kind from him, only a low moaning and the cry, "Water! Water!"

Pala shook with a heavy chill and drew his blanket closer about him. He looked at Teepoo with fear in his eyes.

"Plenty of devils, plenty of devils," the witch doctor remarked as he gazed about the inner room. His keen glance took in the wooden chest by Teejah's sleeping mat. His eyes rested briefly on the brass gongs that hung on the wall. He noted the large size of the rice bin. "Plenty of devils!" He wrinkled his forehead as though in deep thought. "This will take much medicine."

"Oh, Teepoo, use your strongest charms," Teejah wailed. "See how sick they are; use the best medicine you have and drive the devils away."

"I think the devil may be hiding in the big tree by the spring!" Teepoo stepped outside the door and Teejah followed him. "Perhaps if we chop into the tree and make a lot of noise, the evil spirit will be frightened and leave." He walked toward the old tree, drawing his jungle knife from his belt.

"Come, Kasar, help me drive the devil out of this tree," he called to his son, who was loitering in the shade of the hut.

Teejah brought her own jungle knife, and the three of them chopped vigorously at the supporting roots of the tree. It seemed to Teejah like the wounding of an old friend. Surely it was no fault of the tree if devils chose to hide in its branches. Still, this was a desperate circumstance, and they handled their knives with such energy that most of the long supporting roots on one side were cut through. Teepoo stopped every few minutes to shout strong words against the demon.

"I think that should do it," he said at last. "The devil is certainly far away by now." He sheathed his knife, and together the three returned to the house. Teejah hurried up the notched log ladder, full of fear at having been away from the sick boys so long.

"I suppose you will not object to giving me the big brass gong and a few of the chickens?" Teepoo's face twisted into an evil grin.

"Take the gong by all means." Teejah hurried to take it down from the wall. "As for the fowls, take whatever is necessary, but do not touch Pala's black cock."

Teepoo stepped to the door and called Kasar. He took the brass gong and laid it on the boy's shoulders. Kasar went down the notched log ladder, staggering under the weight of the gong. Teepoo descended to the chicken yard and caught one of the hens. He fetched it into the sickroom and began dancing a wild devil dance. At the conclusion he split the body of the fowl with one stroke of his hunting knife and laid it open, bending over it with eager interest to examine the liver and other internal organs.

"The outlook is bad, Teejah." He looked grave. "The omens are not good at all." He drew out some of his charms and rubbed them on the bodies of the boys. Then he began a low chant which grew louder and louder. His body swayed from side to side and at last he fell down in a convulsive fit. When he regained control of himself he had news to impart.

"The spirits are angry with you, Teejah. You must kill one of your water buffalo and make a feast for all the village folk. It seems that the devil has moved closer because we cut the tree. If we have this feast we may be able to find him again and drive him away."

"Take the buffalo that has no calf," Teejah said. "The other one has a small calf, and the calf is Damin's pet."

Teepoo gathered up his things and prepared to go.

"Make haste to help my sons, Teepoo. They are very sick. Arrange the feast for tomorrow." Teejah followed him to the door.

Through the small window of the hut she saw the medicine man help himself to most of her fine hens. Kasar had returned after bearing away the brass gong and was on hand to carry the fowls. She saw Kasar point to the basket on the cottage wall where the black cock was kept, but Teepoo shook his head. Finally the two shuffled off with their hands full of hens.

Teejah turned back to give her full attention to

the boys. Damin had not stirred during all the excitement. Pala's chill had turned to burning fever and he was moaning for water. Teejah hurried to the spring with the empty bamboos, then came back to her place between the two boys. She could not bear to look at the mutilated tree standing lonely and wounded in the evening stillness.

The night drew on again with the usual rainstorm. The water from the broad overhanging eaves of the little hut ran down with a mournful sound that drew hot tears from Teejah's eyes.

There is nothing so cozy as rain on the roof when hearts are warm and cheerful inside a snug dwelling place, but nothing is sadder than falling rain when the heart weeps and hope is dying. So Teejah sat and wept all through that long, dark night, lifting first one boy and then the other to give them drinks of the cool spring water. Toward morning she slept a little from sheer exhaustion. She was wakened by the sound of many voices and footsteps around the house. Then she remembered that this was the day of the feast.

"Peaceful morning to you, Teejah." The women of the village crowded into the sickroom.

Teejah pointed to the rice bin. The women took measure after measure of the padi and began to pound out the rice for the feast. They had brought along several of the wooden mortars used in hulling the rice. Each mortar was a thick length of log, wide at the base and hollowed deeply from the top. Two women worked at one mortar. With long poles they kept up a rhythmic pounding until the husks were separated from the rice.

Other women poured the beaten padi into large winnowing baskets, fanning and tossing it in the light breeze until the husks were blown away and only the plump kernels of rice remained. It took a lot of rice for the feast, but there were many helpers and the work was soon done. The rice was boiled in a number of iron pots over wood fires.

Meanwhile, the men had been busy with the butchering. The water buffalo was now hung from the stout branch of the big old tree by the spring, and they were slicing off slabs of flesh to be boiled

82   MIRACLE OF THE SONG

in huge caldrons. Other helpers from the village had invaded the widow's store of rice wine and had contributed some of their own so that the feast should lack nothing. As the hot day wore on, more and more people came to join the feast and partake of the good things offered to the spirits.

Teepoo was everywhere, taking part in all the activities. He superintended the preparation of the

food, and when the dancing and drinking began no one was so noisy and excited as he.

Teejah still sat between the two boys. The sounds of the feast drowned the little hut in a tumult of noise. The boys moaned constantly and turned their heads from side to side. Teejah wondered if the loud noises were distressing them, but surely this was the only thing to do, the only way

to get relief. Perhaps the spirits would relent and reveal the hiding place of the devil who was causing all this trouble. Often she arose from her place and stood at the little window to watch the activity of the crowd outside.

Teepoo was ready to perform his incantations. A spirit tent had been made for him out of the fresh fronds of new coconut leaves. It hung like a teepee from another branch of the tree where the buffalo carcass was swinging. As the witch doctor danced, he often whirled into the spirit tent, and loud, breathy noises issued from it. "Shush-sh-shshshsh!"

Louder and louder, more and more furious grew the dance. At length the witch doctor fell over in a trancelike stupor. At this all the people who had been hilarious with excitement fell silent and waited in stifled terror for the fit to pass.

The witch doctor sprang to his feet with a wild scream. "The devil! The devil! He is in the water spring, the water spring! Do you hear? The devil is in the water spring!"

The crowd looked and listened in stupid silence.

"Come, you!" Teepoo shrieked. "Get to the spring! Destroy it! Stop it up! Destroy the dwelling place of the devil, and he will depart."

There was movement in the crowd. With one accord they hurried to the spring. The neat bamboo trough was jerked out and stamped in the mud. The stones so carefully placed by Damin and Pala were thrown in every direction. Dirt and mud were clawed over the bubbling water in wild haste. When they had finished, the litter of rubbish was heaped so high that no one would have guessed that this morning a flowing stream of clear, cool water had gushed there from the low hillside into a smooth basin of stones.

Teejah watched this demonstration with excited relief. Yes, it must be the spring where the devil was lurking. They visited the spring so often, and the boys often rested there in the heat of the day. Yes, surely Teepoo was right. He was a clever witch doctor, sure enough. Now, without doubt, everything would take a turn for the better. It was well worth the sacrifice of the water buffalo and the annoyance of the noisy feast. Now the trouble had been located and remedied. The villagers had done their full duty. They had enjoyed the feast and now they prepared to depart, each for his own hut in the village.

When they had all gone, Teejah bent over the sick boys. There was still no outward change in their appearance. Both of them stirred in their delirium and begged for water. With trembling hands she gathered up the empty water bamboos and crept down the notched log ladder in the dusk. Where could she go now for water? The spring was stopped. The place must be forever avoided in the future. Where could she fill the bamboos with water to cool the parched throats of the sick lads? She remembered the ditch along the border of the rice fields. It would be running full to the brim with water. True, it was fed from the buffalo wallows above, but nothing could be done about that now. She ran to the ditch, filled the bamboos, and hurried back to the hut. The rain began to fall as it did every night at this season of the year.

At sunrise the next morning Majang appeared

at the foot of the ladder. "I suppose the boys are better today," he called up to Teejah.

"I can see no change." Teejah stood at the top of the ladder in the open door.

"I heard that Teepoo located the devil in the water spring. That was clever of him." Majang came up the ladder. He came into the inner room and looked down at the two boys. Oh, they were very sick indeed!

"Teejah," he said gravely, "it is possible that more than one devil is involved in this trouble. Perhaps Teepoo should come back and look into the matter again." He shook his head with concern.

Teejah sat with a hand on each of her sons and wept without restraint. Majang, uneasy and embarrassed, backed toward the door. "I'll tend to the chickens and round up the water buffalo for you," he said as he departed.

"Stop at Teepoo's place and tell him to come over again, Majang. I have no one else to send." Teejah followed him to the door and called after him as he was leaving.

It was late afternoon when the witch doctor came again to the widow's hut. "It is possible that the spirits are angry because there was not sufficient offering made," he suggested. "I will try the spirits again and see if I can find out what the trouble is." He squatted on the floor in an attitude of complete indifference.

"Name your fee, Teepoo, and you shall have it." Teejah held out both hands to him in a supplicating gesture.

"Well, I will take the rest of the fowls. You have no time to feed them any more. I would like some rolls of cloth from your chest, as I am in need of new clothing. You are wearing some choice beads, too. I am sure it would please the spirits if you made a sacrifice of those beads."

Teejah drew the beads from around her neck as she went to open the wooden chest. She placed four rolls of choice red and black cloth in Teepoo's arms and took the other brass gong from the wall. He hurried down the ladder as fast as he could with such a load and carried the things home. Then he returned for the chickens. By the time the chickens were safely deposited in the witch doctor's henyard it was dark and no more incantations could be performed that day.

Teejah took the water bamboos and went down to the ditch to fill them. When she returned she noticed that the black cock's basket was gone. It no longer hung under the eaves. So Kasar had accomplished his purpose at last. Her eyes filled with hot tears.

When Teepoo came the following day and went through his incantations, he said that another feast must be held. It must be bigger and better than the first. Teepoo offered to take the three remaining water buffalo and a large amount of padi in exchange for a very large buffalo which would make, he said, a magnificent offering to the spirits.

So it was arranged. The villagers, always glad of any opportunity for feasting, co-operated in every way possible. The wild excitement of the second feast matched anything the village had ever known in the way of festive hilarity.

When the food had been enjoyed and the ceremonies to placate the spirits had been completed, Teepoo took up the task of locating the devil. With wild contortions and ferocious screams, he set about this delicate business, finally announcing the startling news that the devil had again been found.

"In the beam! In the beam, men!" he screamed. "In the central beam of the house, do you hear?" They heard, but were for the moment too para-

lyzed to act. "Tear it out! Tear it out!" He urged them on.

The strongest men of the village scrambled up the ladder into the house. Many rough hands grabbed the offending timber. They twisted and wrenched it, pulling with all their combined strength, until with a great heave they brought the beam away with a portion of the roof hanging to it. It was hauled outside with demonstrations of triumph and great joy. Now, at last, the offending demon had been outwitted! The villagers returned home, satisfied that they had done their duty by the widow and her two sons. Things would certainly be better after this.

The rain began again and fell all night. Teejah pulled the two mats as far as possible from the gaping hole in the roof and brought sheets of *kajang* to shelter the boys. Neither was conscious. Teejah kept her lonely watch through the long night. The rain fell faster and faster and poured in streams from the wide eaves of the little hut and through the hole in the broken roof.

6. All Is Not Enough

"I wondered all night if you and the boys could keep dry." It was Majang, who had come in the early dawn. He looked about the place, soaked and disordered. Teejah had protected the two boys as well as she could and had spread *kajang* over the rice bin to save the rice—what was left of it after the two feasts.

"The boys are no better." Teejah sat between them, her face drawn and weary with constant watching and black despair. "They don't even call for water any more. I think they will both die." The brokenhearted mother bowed her head and the hot tears fell on her clenched hands.

"I think it might be good to call that new teacher from Buluno Village," Majang urged her gently.

"He has pity for the sick and his medicine is powerful."

Teejah raised her two hands in a gesture of annoyance. "No, Majang, it is too late now for me to change medicine. We must call Teepoo back. Go quickly and tell him I will give everything I have left if he will come once more and try to rid us of the demons that are killing my sons."

Reluctantly Majang left the broken little hut and went up through the village. It was nearly noon when the witch doctor again showed himself at the widow's door. He called a cheerful greeting and walked in.

"The spirits are certainly angry with you, Teejah." He looked at the two unconscious boys, at the torn roof, the wet floor, and the widow's stricken face. "There must be some reason for all this. You must have kept back whatever it is that the spirits want most."

"Take it all, take everything!" Teejah lifted her voice in a shrill scream. "What good is anything to me without my sons?" She flew to the wooden chest and emptied it. Teepoo's avaricious eyes rested lovingly on the treasures concealed so long, but now brought forth to pay his fee: old fine weavings, rolls of cloth, sarongs, even a few lengths of rare Brunei gold cloth. All were dumped on the mat and Teejah showed him that the chest was empty. Then she stripped her arms and ankles of the jewelry she had worn since girlhood. "Here

is the padi bin. Take what you want!" She pulled away the *kajang* coverings and drew out woven grass bags for him to fill.

"This is very good, Teejah. I am sure the spirits will regard you with kindness this time. I will arrange the feast for tomorrow." Gathering up as much of the booty as he could carry, he fumbled his way to the door and departed. In an hour he returned with Kasar, and together they were able to clear away the rest of the offering. Kasar staggered under a huge bag of padi.

"I think there will be enough rice for the feast," Teepoo reassured Teejah as he departed.

All night the mother worked over the two boys. She tried to feed them hot rice gruel. She gave them water. She rubbed their cold bodies with a liniment made from coconut oil mixed with hot chillies, bruised in a stone mortar.

The third feast was much like the two previous ones. The village people came willingly to partake of the freshly killed water buffalo, for Teepoo had provided one himself this time. The rice bin contained enough for the large crowd, and by noon

Teepoo was pursuing his incantations and devil-seeking in a loud and violent manner. His wild dancing and chanting and convulsive fits finally came to an abrupt end. Rising to his feet in an attitude of terrible defiance, he screamed, "Oh, clever devil! Oh, clever devil! We have you! We have you at last!"

Everyone craned their necks and crowded close to see where the devil could be hiding this time. "To the hut! To the hut!" he shrieked, and led the way into the cottage himself. As many of the villagers as could crowd in followed him. He bent over the sick boys, first Damin, then Pala.

"Here! Here!" He leaped with wild excitement. "The devil is in Pala's front teeth." With another leap and flourish he sank down on the floor, too exhausted by the orgies of the week to endure more.

The strong men of the village gathered around. What a place for a devil to hide himself! Teejah considered the situation thoughtfully. There was nothing to do but get rid of the teeth. No more help could be expected from Teepoo today. Everyone could see that. His friends dragged him down the ladder and away to his own hut.

Teejah turned to the other men. "Will one of you take a stone and knock out Pala's teeth?" she begged.

"We are not skilled in knocking out teeth," one of them explained. "The boy is quite sick. It might make him feel much worse to have his teeth knocked out."

Everyone agreed that a serious and difficult situation had arisen. It was then that Majang came forward, hesitantly, as though driven by forces over which he himself had no control.

"There is a new witch man come to our village, as most of you know. There is a white Tuan who helps him with things like this. The Tuan has pinching things of iron that he fastens onto a tooth and it pops right out. What do you think? Is it good that I should call this young man, Rindoo, and his master, the white Tuan?"

"This new witchcraft of Rindoo is dangerous,"

ALL IS NOT ENOUGH

one of the village men answered. "If one eats the medicine of this young man, or if one listens to his talk, or if one allows him to lay a hand on one's body, then the heart flies away. It is taken like a bird in a trap and the heart goes with Rindoo." The villagers shook their heads. It was a desperate situation.

"Which one of you will knock Pala's teeth out?" Teejah faced them with dark anger in her eyes. "Which one of you will rid us of the devils? I have nothing left to pay Teepoo to make more medicine. Go, Majang, call this new witch man and the white Tuan. Things cannot be worse than they are." Teejah's voice trembled and her whole body shook with fear. This was an awful decision to make. Majang hastened away, and one by one the village people straggled home. Not all of them left. Some waited to see if the new witch man would come. Buluno Village was not far away, not more than an hour's walking through the rice fields.

"Elder Sister," a cheerful voice called that afternoon from the door of the hut, "may we come in and help you?" Teejah looked up and saw Majang bringing the young man, Rindoo, into the house.

"Come in," Teejah murmured, in a voice so low it was scarcely more than a whisper. "Come in and help us, if there is any help for us."

The young man, Rindoo, wore clothes of spotless white. His large brown eyes held a depth of compassionate kindness that Teejah had never seen before in anyone's eyes. He knelt between the two boys. He felt their hands. He examined their stomachs. He lifted the lids of their eyes and peered into them.

"Tell me about this sickness," he encouraged Teejah. The kindness in his voice seemed to loosen a torrent of words. With a flood of tears and excited gestures Teejah told the whole story of the sickness and the feasts and the devil that moved about from one place to another. She explained the reason for the open hole in the roof, the empty rice bin, the vacant henyard, the empty wooden chest; she told about the stopped-up water spring.

"Now help us if you can!" She pointed to Pala, still lying senseless on his mat. "The devil has crawled into his front teeth and we have no way of removing the teeth." Teejah settled herself back on the mat, appalled by what she had done. She had given her complete confidence to this young stranger. But there was no proof at all that he was going to be able to help. It was likely that she had incurred the everlasting displeasure of the spirits. She would never be forgiven for this, never! She buried her face in her hands and wept without restraint.

"Do not grieve, Elder Sister." Rindoo spoke gently. "I am sure we can help you. This boy's teeth look all right to me, but I have sent for the Tuan. He will be here in a little while, and if the teeth are causing trouble he can take them out with no difficulty." Rindoo stroked Pala's forehead as he talked. "I have some medicine with me that will help the boys." He drew a glass bottle from his coat pocket. "It is very bitter. We may have some trouble getting them to swallow it, but it will quickly destroy the fever that is devouring them."

Majang hurried to bring a coconut cup. Rindoo

poured half the contents of the bottle into the cup and held it to Pala's lips. The boy was too sick to make much objection, and Rindoo was skilled in administering such doses. He poured the remainder out for Damin. With some urging he persuaded him to swallow his portion.

"This sickness is caused by mosquitoes." Rindoo still sat between the two boys. The widow had calmed herself a little and the young teacher spoke in a low voice. "In this place where there is always much water there are also many mosquitoes. Each mosquito has a small spear which he uses to pierce our bodies. The spear is hollow, like a tube, and through it he sucks out blood. That is painful, but it is not the worst thing the mosquito does. He also blows back into our bodies the blood from his own small body." Rindoo waited to see if Teejah understood. She listened with eager attention. Something about the young man took hold of her heart. She felt herself believing his words.

"If one person in a house has the sickness in his blood and a mosquito sucks from him and then goes on to another, he can carry the sickness from person to person until a whole village may get it."

"We have always been taught that the devils make the sickness." Teejah spoke with what reserve she could command. This new witchcraft was peculiar. Still, she remembered the swarms of mosquitoes that flew in clouds around the water spring and the open ditches of water. She knew that every home in the village was plagued with fever at some time or other. Many persons died with it. Her own husband, the father of Damin and Pala, had died just so.

Teejah was still considering what Rindoo had said when voices were heard outside. The Tuan had arrived and with him a number of the village folk who were eager to see how the white man would dispose of the devils in Pala's front teeth.

Majang sprang to open the door and welcome the Tuan. As the tall man entered the hut he looked in amazement at the torn roof and the twisted floor where the timber had been torn out. He looked inquiringly at Rindoo, but it was

Majang who spoke. "Make yourself comfortable," he said. He fetched a mat and the Tuan, who had left his shoes at the door, settled himself.

He was a tall, thin man. Teejah looked at his hands. They were the largest man's hands she had ever seen. His face was almost as dark as Rindoo's, but his features were different. His nose was long, his chin strong and thrust forward. His gray eyes were large and deep-set. His voice was soft and gentle. Teejah relaxed. Fear of the anger of the spirits left her. She had no doubt any more that the medicine these two could make would be of value.

Then suddenly she remembered. "I am very sorry." She looked into the Tuan's gray eyes. "I have nothing left to give you for your medicine. I have given all to Teepoo, but it was not enough."

"This medicine we bring is of a different kind," Rindoo assured her with a smile. "I have just given both the boys a dose of liquid quinine," he explained to the Tuan. Then he related the whole pitiful story of the boys' long illness, the witch feasts, the elusive devil, and the need for the teeth to be knocked out.

The white man leaned forward in grave concern. Then he examined the teeth of both boys as well as their arms and legs and stomachs and backs. He saw the fresh burn on Damin's chest, and Rindoo asked Teejah what had happened.

"We often try to burn the devils out," she explained. "Sometimes one thing will work and sometimes another. We have to try all the different ways if the devil keeps staying around."

"This boy's teeth are perfect." The Tuan finished his examination. "They don't need to be pulled. By tomorrow morning you will see that both boys will be much better. Rindoo will come again tomorrow with more of the medicine. In a few days the boys will be walking around."

"Tell me, why do you make medicine for people without asking payment?" Teejah searched the faces of the two visitors. The villagers who had crowded into the room waited eagerly for the answer.

"Look toward the mountain." Rindoo indicated the open door, through which all of them could see the majestic form of Mount Kinabalu rising above the nearer hills. "Look at the sky. See the sun that gives light to all of us. Consider all the trees, the rivers, the animals, even the people themselves. Where did they all come from?"

This unexpected question closed every mouth. Where, indeed? Who could know the answer to such a question? The village people grunted and chewed their quids of betel nut and said nothing. Teejah had never heard such matters discussed. The mountain, the river, the rice fields, the water buffalo, and the people had always been there, so far as she knew.

"There is a great God who made all these things." Rindoo looked around at all of them and pulled a small black book from his coat pocket. "This is the Word of the great God of Heaven, who made all these things. It is He who tells us to love one another and do all the kindness we can to everyone."

At sight of the black book the village people nudged one another. Some of them crept furtively toward the door. This was the book about which they had all heard. This was the book that changed people into different creatures. Teejah looked at it in fascinated wonder.

Rindoo opened the book and read: "Whatsoever, therefore, ye would that men should do to you, do ye even so to them."

The visitors rose to go. "May we speak for a moment to the great God who sent us here?" Rindoo asked Teejah. She looked into his eyes without comprehension. The two men lifted their faces, and Rindoo spoke as to a close and beloved friend. "Oh, Father of us all, bless and comfort this mother and, if it be your will, make these two boys well from their fever. Our love to you! Our love to you! Thank you! Thank you!"

In the stunned silence that followed this prayer the two men left the hut and disappeared down the path in the early twilight. Majang went with them. The villagers came and looked at the two

boys. Such strange medicine had never been made in the village. As they left the hut Teejah could hear them arguing and discussing the possibility of good or of evil, filled with wonderment at the strange things they had seen and heard and with curiosity about the medicine and its possible results.

Late in the night Pala moved on his mat. "Mother," he called in a weak voice. "I am hungry. Bring me food."

7. The Curse of Teepoo

EARLY THE FOLLOWING MORNING Majang appeared. Rain had fallen in the night and Teejah's hut, broken and drenched, was no cozy place to look at, but joy was there.

"I knew it!" Majang's face beamed. "I knew that Rindoo would help them." He looked at the two boys. Pala was eating rice gruel which Teejah fed him. Damin lay asleep, but his breathing was natural. Anyone could see that both boys were better. For the first time in many days Teejah's heart was comforted.

"Peaceful morning to you," Rindoo called, as he came hurrying up the notched log ladder into the hut. It was no surprise to him to find the boys free of fever. Majang brought water and the coconut cup. Again the young teacher poured the bitter medicine and persuaded the boys to take it.

"They must have it three times today," Rindoo ordered. "You may give it to them at noon, and I will return at sundown." He measured a portion for Damin into one bottle and another equal portion into a second bottle for Pala.

Teejah put the precious medicine up on top of the rice bin, then turned to her new friend with a heart so full of gratitude that words would not come to express what she felt. But Rindoo seemed to understand.

"If you are willing," he said, looking at her kindly, "Majang and I will clear the rubbish from the spring today." Teejah hesitated. "It is not good to drink the water from the ditch," Rindoo went on. "The boys might get sickness of the stomach."

"You don't believe any more that the devil is in the spring," Majang persuaded her.

"No. I believe what the teacher has said—that the mosquito has brought the sickness." Teejah spoke in a low voice. She felt almost frightened at her own words. This was rank defiance of the evil spirits.

"Then the spring is harmless. May we make it nice for you again?" Rindoo pressed her for an answer.

Teejah nodded her head. "Do," she whispered. "I will be grateful to you for doing it."

When Teepoo came to inquire after the boys he looked past the twisted little house to the hillside, where two energetic young men were digging and scraping the rubbish from the spring. Teejah, who was watching him from the window of the hut, noted the expression on his face and knew that he was shocked and angry. Her heart beat fast as she opened the door.

Teepoo walked past her into the inner room. He stood looking down at the two boys. "Aha! The fever is gone." His eyes brightened.

"Yes. I called the new teacher from Buluno Village and the Tuan who helps him. This is the second day the boys have taken his medicine." As Teejah spoke, her courage grew. "The teacher is helping Majang clean the spring for us today."

Teepoo's dark eyes glittered. He looked first at Damin, then at Pala, then at their mother. "Foolish woman!" he cried in hot anger. "How dare you bring the foreign witchcraft to our village! The spirits are angry with you! A curse is on your house!"

So Teepoo spoke in his wrath and then departed. But, strangely enough, Teejah was not afraid. She was beginning to believe in the magic of the black book and in the strong and bitter medicine of the white Tuan.

By the middle of the morning the spring was cleaned and restored. A new bamboo trough flowed with clear, cool water, and the fall of the stream on the basin of smooth stones made pleasant music. Teejah came now with the water bamboos on her shoulder and filled them.

"Keep it this way"—Rindoo washed his hands in the flowing water—"and you will always have pure, clean water to drink. That is very important if one is to avoid sickness."

"The next thing is the house." Majang looked toward the hut. "I doubt if that house can be repaired, it is so twisted out of shape."

"Perhaps we can plan something tomorrow." Rindoo smiled his engaging smile. "Maybe we shall have to build a new house."

"Oh, no! No!" Teejah cried. "We have nothing at all left. How can we build a new house? It is not even to be thought of." She picked up the full bamboos, then turned to face the two men. "I do not mind living in a broken house, now that my boys are getting well."

Rindoo and Majang went home to Buluno Village. Teejah stood the full bamboos in the kitchen room of the hut. Then she made everything as tidy as possible and opened the rice bin. There was very little left after the three feasts and Teepoo's heavy fee. She took a long whisk of coconut-leaf ribs and swept the bin, gathering all the remaining padi into a pile in the middle. Then with great care she picked up every grain, threw it into the mortar where she always pounded out the rice, and began the work of hulling the last measure of padi.

"Mother, Mother," Pala was calling. "Why does Damin sleep all the time and not talk?"

"Damin was sick longer than you, Pala," his mother explained. "He is all right. He can eat now and the fever is gone."

Teejah went back to her padi-pounding. Her heart had been light when she talked to the men at the spring. Now, as she looked at her scanty measure of rice and thought of the two boys who were beginning to eat again, she became discouraged. How could the boys get well if they had no rice to eat?

She finished hulling the padi and winnowed it by tossing it in a flat scoop-shaped basket. The light breeze carried away the husks. She poured the hulled rice in a tight basket and went outside the hut again.

The yellow orchid still hung on the side of the house. It had flourished in the constant rains. More of the blooms had opened. Teejah carefully took down the plant, carried it into the hut, and set it down between the two boys. The peculiar beauty of the yellow blossoms spotted with brown brought a light to Pala's eyes. He sat up on his mat and reached pale hands for the orchid. He touched it with soft, inquiring fingers—not the delicate blossoms, but the glossy, shining leaves.

"Oh, Mother, it is beautiful!" he said.

"Yes, it makes the heart glad to see it," Teejah admitted. "Do you know that Teacher Rindoo says the God of Heaven made all the flowers and trees, the plants and animals?"

"Will Rindoo come again today?" Pala asked.

"He will come this evening," Teejah assured him. "But now you must take the medicine, for the sun is at midheaven." She brought water and the coconut cup and fed them both the bitter medicine. Damin had to be wakened. He made no objection to the medicine. Teejah set the orchid where the light from the little window would fall on it and tried to call his attention to it, but he looked at the plant with listless, indifferent eyes. Then he went back to sleep again.

That evening when Rindoo called, "Peace to you," from the door of the hut, Pala answered, with a welcoming smile, "Peace to your coming."

"You are much better this evening." The young teacher looked pleased. Then as he sat down cross-legged on the mat he noticed the yellow orchid. "Where did you get such a lovely orchid? I have never seen so fine a one."

Pala sat up on his mat and told Rindoo about Damin's trip to Togop Village and the finding of the yellow orchid.

Rindoo looked closely at Damin and held his hand for a long time. "Does he eat?" The teacher bent to listen, with his ear against the boy's naked chest.

"He eats." Teejah set the orchid at the other side of the room. "He eats and he takes the bitter medicine, but he sleeps much and talks little."

"I think he is weak from the long fever," the teacher reassured her. "It will take a little more time for him to recover."

After the medicine was given, Rindoo spoke words to the God of Heaven, asking for his help in the healing of the boys. Then he took out the black book and read from it. Teejah could not understand all the words, but they said that if even a small ricebird fell to the ground, the God of Heaven would know. They said that He had counted the hairs on the heads of all the people.

"How many teeth has Pala got?" Rindoo closed the black book and put it back in his pocket.

"I don't know." Teejah looked at him in surprise.

"You love your son so much." Rindoo looked at Pala with deep affection in his face. "You love your son so much, and yet you have never counted his teeth?"

Teejah searched his face. "Why is it important, Teacher?" She could not understand.

"You, who love your son, do not know the number of his teeth, but the God of Heaven, who loves us all, has counted even the hairs of our heads." Rindoo waited while Teejah turned this over in her mind. "Do you see? He loves us so much more."

Then Rindoo spoke of other things. He asked about the rice bin. Did they have enough for the season? Teejah, being full of pride, answered, "We still have some left."

The rain began then and Rindoo frowned as he looked at the broken roof. He tucked the red blankets tightly around the two boys and helped Teejah arrange the sheets of *kajang* to shut out as much of the rain as possible.

"Has Teepoo come to visit you today?" Rindoo stood in the door ready to go. "Was he angry?"

"He was angry." Teejah lifted grave eyes. "He cursed me and my boys and my house, but I am without fear."

"Remember, the God of Heaven loves you." The young man raised his hand to heaven. "Even the hairs of your heads are all counted."

After he had gone, Teejah carried the orchid out into the rain and hung it on the side of the house, where it had been ever since Damin brought it from Togop. The rain increased and the night came down, black and cheerless. Teejah rolled up in her damp blanket and thought about the curse of Teepoo, but then she remembered the words from the black book: "Even the hairs of your head are all counted." And her heart was unafraid.

Majang came in the early morning. "Where do you want the new house to stand?" he asked her.

"We cannot have a new house." Teejah was firm.

"Look now. Rindoo and I planned it last night. This house is almost new. The *attap* on the roof is still good, also the *kajang* in the walls. The bamboo of the floor is mostly usable. We need only the timbers for the frame, and the big one they tore out is still lying out here."

"But that will require much work." Teejah was still resisting.

"There will be friends who will be glad to do the work." Majang smiled mysteriously.

Then Teejah talked of Teepoo and his curse and of many other things, but she did not tell Majang that the rice bin was empty and that there was only enough rice to last one more day.

"That orchid is loaded with blossoms!" Majang lifted the plant from its place on the outside wall of the hut. The glossy leaves glistened in the early sunshine. He set it on the ladder and admired it.

"I have a thought." Majang laughed and slapped his knee. "Today a great ship lies off the jetty in Jesselton. It came in this morning and it will go out tonight. It always comes every week on this day."

"What has the great ship to do with this orchid?" Teejah was puzzled.

"Sometimes the big Tuans travel on the ship. If they should see that orchid plant, I am sure they would want it. They want these plants in order to make them grow in their own houses." Majang slapped his knee again. "Why didn't I think of it before?"

Teejah's heart lifted. "Take it and go at once," she urged. "The way is long, but the day is just begun."

So Majang lifted the gorgeous plant and started off at a brisk trot for the road two miles away where he could get a bus to carry him to the seaport town where the great ship lay moored.

Teejah watched him go with a lightness of heart she tried to resist; for what right had she to feel lighthearted with no rice in the bin, no hens in the yard, no buffalo to plow the rice field, and only a broken, twisted hut to live in through the rainy season? But the shining thing in her heart refused to be denied.

On this day Damin sat on his mat and ate by himself from his rice bowl. Teejah talked to him, but he only looked at her with vacant, indifferent eyes and mumbled to himself.

Rindoo brought the medicine as usual. When he came at sundown he looked long at Damin and shook his head in grave concern.

"What is it, Teacher?" Teejah searched his face.

"I don't really know." Rindoo stroked Damin's pale hand. "It seems to me that he should be different than he is. I will ask the Tuan to come. He will know."

The young teacher read again from the black book about God's care for the small ricebirds and how the hairs of our heads are all counted; and how He clothes the flowers and the grass in bright garments, but His people are more to Him than the grass and flowers and birds.

Then Rindoo left and peace came back to Teejah's heart. She talked with Pala about Majang and his journey into Jesselton with the yellow orchid.

"Tomorrow I will go outside and walk about," Pala announced. "And I will play with my black cock and Damin's baby buffalo."

Teejah felt a hurt deep inside. "Oh, Pala," she said, "the water buffalo are gone, and the black cock is gone, and the padi is gone. I gave them all to Teepoo so he would make medicine."

Pala drew the red blanket over his head and sobbed, and his mother sat by him and patted him through the blanket while the tears streamed down her own cheeks. Damin roused a little, looked vaguely troubled, and mumbled softly to himself, but Teejah could not understand what he was trying to say.

Then Pala threw off the blanket and saw his

mother's wet eyes and her sadness. "Don't feel sorry, Mother," he said. "As soon as I am well I will work hard and buy us more water buffalo and more chickens." In the comfort of this resolution Pala went to sleep.

8. The Fallen Sparrow

AT SUNRISE Majang came with a merry face. Teejah was boiling the last of the rice for the boys' breakfast when he clambered up the ladder and stuck his head in the door, shouting, "Peaceful morning to you!"

"Oh, Majang!" Teejah jerked most of the burning sticks from under the rice pot. "Did you sell it? Tell us about it."

Majang fumbled with a hard knot in the tail of his loincloth. He finally got the knot untied and produced a closely folded wad of paper money. He unfolded the money and shook it between his fingers. "I got to the ship at noon." He could not sit down for his great excitement, but paced about the room as he talked. "The sun was at midheaven.

I was glad, because the plant was unhurt. Every flower was perfect. The people from the boat were all scattered through the town, but I heard that the ship was to sail at five o'clock, so I squatted in the shade of the boat and waited."

Majang shook the money again and smiled. "It was almost time for the ship to sail when the people began to come back. I was squatting right by the ladder they must all use to climb up into the ship, so they could all see me and the flowers. The first Tuan and his lady stopped and admired the orchid and offered me a dollar for it, but I laughed at him and said I must have twenty-five dollars. By that time other Tuans and ladies had gathered. They all thought the flowers were rare and beautiful. They were excited. The first Tuan kept offering me more and more. I was about to let him have it for fifteen dollars when the officer of the ship shouted in a loud and angry voice, 'All aboard!' I heard the ringing of a bell. Then a tall Tuan who had been standing back of the others sprang forward, thrust this wad of money into my hand, and took the plant. He ran up the ladder with it before I realized what had happened." Majang paused to catch his breath. "When I counted the money it was really twenty-five dollars." He shook the money again.

"Twenty-five dollars! Twenty-five dollars!" Teejah gasped in an awed voice. "But it is yours, Majang. You went to the mountain for the orchid and you made that long journey yesterday."

Majang was firm. He insisted that he had given the yellow orchid to Damin and he would not take one cent of the money.

"Has anyone in Buluno Village got padi for sale?" Teejah followed him to the door as he started down the ladder.

"I will find out," he answered. Then he paused and understanding spread over his troubled face. "So Teepoo took all the padi, too. All the padi!"

Majang looked as if he had just swallowed a thorny fish. He muttered some words under his breath that Teejah scarcely heard, but she understood that Majang was angry. Even now he did not know that she had cooked the very last of the hulled rice.

The Tuan came with Rindoo that day, and both men looked for a long time at Damin. His fever had been gone for some days now. He could eat and sleep, but he had no wish to do anything else. He mumbled noises that no one could understand, and in his eyes was no light, only a dull vacancy of expression.

"He had the fever so long." Rindoo knelt beside Damin's mat.

The Tuan looked so grave that Teejah's heart began to pound. "What is it, Tuan?" She must know; she must understand.

"We will wait a few more days." The Tuan spoke with much kindness. "Then if he is no better we may take him to the hospital in Jesselton to see the Tuan doctor there."

"Our people say that all who go to the hospital either die or are bewitched." Teejah was greatly troubled.

"No, no." The Tuan smiled. "Many people are cured of sickness in the hospital, and most of those who die would have lived if they had gone to the hospital sooner."

After the two men had gone, the widow knelt for a long time by her older son. So the curse of Teepoo had fallen after all, and the fine, bright lad would never be anything but an idiot, a body without a mind. She wept until no tears were left, and Pala tried in vain to comfort her. It was hours later in the night when Teejah remembered that she had made no supper for Pala. There was no rice to give him.

Next morning the sun rose as clear and beautiful as though there were no sadness and no heavy hearts in all the land. There was no change in Damin's condition. From that dark place where his soul wandered now, what chance was there that he might be brought back? Teejah remembered the story of the little boy lost on the dark mountain. Could some prayer be directed to the God of Heaven so that this lost one might be brought back?

So Teejah mused to herself as she picked up the bamboos and went to the spring to fill them. When she returned, there inside the hut lay a small bag. Teejah hardly dared to touch it. Could it be rice? At last she touched the bag and then snatched it up. It was rice, hulled rice! Who could have brought it? Surely no one knew of the empty rice bin. Even Majang did not know that she had cooked the last of her supply of rice yesterday. Yet here was this bag of rice, set just inside her door.

"Every hair of your head is counted." The words came back to Teejah with the force of a living voice. Comfort and peace flowed into her heart, and she washed rice and prepared the morning meal with great thankfulness. Pala came into the kitchen room of the hut and ate his breakfast with hearty appetite. Then he ran out into the village.

Damin ate too. But although his body grew

stronger every day, he seemed to notice nothing and to care nothing about what went on around him.

In the middle of the forenoon Rindoo, Majang, and four other men appeared, carrying heavy timbers. They laid the beams down and began to mark out a rectangle on the ground to the side and a little back of Teejah's hut.

"Come out." Majang stood at the foot of the ladder, wiping the perspiration from his eyes with the back of his hand. "Come and hear what we have planned for the house."

"We have three beams besides this one of yours." Rindoo indicated the central timber that had been torn out to get rid of the devil. "There are five more to bring and we are going after them now."

Teejah was bewildered. What did it mean? Who were these strangers who were willing to carry heavy timbers in the hot sun for a penniless widow they had never seen?

"These are some of the believers from Buluno."

Rindoo read her thought. "They know about your troubles. I have told them. They are glad to help build your house. It will not take long."

Majang explained that they would erect the frame and put on a roof of new *attap*. Then they would tear off the *kajang* sheets from the walls of the broken hut and the bamboo from the floor.

"We will move you into the new house and then use the frame and roof of this hut to make a large veranda on the new one," Majang explained, gesturing with his hands as he talked. So the building was staked out after careful measuring and the

work began that very day. Six determined men can do a lot on a simple thatched house in one day.

"Oh, Mother!" Pala hurried into the hut that evening. "What are the men building?"

"Come, eat your rice and I will tell you all about it." Teejah filled his plate and went to fetch Damin from the inner room, so that he might sit and eat with his brother. Pala was excited as well as hungry. "Oh, Mother, Teepoo is full of anger at us. He says that because of your calling Rindoo to make medicine in our house Damin has been cursed and he will never be anything but a stupid fool."

"I am sure Teepoo believes that we are under the curse of the spirits. But I do not believe it. I believe what is written in the black book. The God of Heaven cares for us so much that even the hairs of our heads are all counted." Teejah's courage rose as she talked to Pala.

"Kasar is winning all the cockfights in the village with my black cock." Pala spoke with a bitterness that he could not conceal.

Teejah laid a gentle hand on her son's arm. "Do not feel sad, Pala. I think cockfighting is cruel and maybe a little silly. It starts so many quarrels among the boys and men."

Then they talked of the new house and how wonderful it would be to live in such a fine place. At last they went to their sleeping mats.

"Mother, I am going to help the men build the house." Pala hurried through his breakfast the following morning.

"Oh, that is good," his mother rejoiced. "There must be many things you can do to help."

When the men appeared, Majang was carrying a *bohongan* full of padi. He brought it up the ladder and threw open the lid of the rice bin. A look of surprise passed over his face as he saw that the bin was empty, clean and swept. He dumped the contents of the *bohongan* into the bin, shaking out the last grains with such spiteful vigor that Teejah smiled.

"Do you know who brought the bag of hulled

rice and set it inside my door yesterday morning?" Teejah studied Majang's face.

"Yes, I brought it," Majang answered. "It is mountain rice. I traded some coconuts for it, and I thought it might be a treat for you and the boys."

"Then you knew that we had nothing to cook for breakfast?" Teejah asked.

"I did not know." Majang and Teejah looked into each other's eyes for a long moment. Teejah knew that he was thinking her thoughts. Both were thinking of the words of the black book and of the love of the God of Heaven for his people.

It was amazing how fast the new house grew. The timbers were soon in place and the new *attap* tied on. From some unknown source came bamboo for the floor, all flattened and seasoned.

"Tomorrow I think you can move in." Rindoo finished setting a notched log ladder at the door of the new house. "It isn't done yet, but we can use the material in this hut to finish it after you are moved in."

"It is a fine house." Teejah looked it over with pride. "But I shall never consider it my own. It will always belong to those who have need of shelter and those who wish to listen to the words from the book of the God of Heaven."

"Will you be willing for us to take Damin to the hospital tomorrow?" Rindoo put the question with kindness and waited for the answer with such sympathy in his face that it brought tears to Teejah's eyes.

"He may go," she declared with simple faith, "if you will go with him."

"I will go," the teacher hastened to assure her. "The Tuan will go too, for he is a friend of the doctor at the hospital."

The following day, in the midst of the excitement of moving into the new house, the Tuan and Rindoo came to take Damin to the hospital. It was not known whether the doctor would keep him at the hospital for several days or send him back at once, so it was with eager interest that Pala and his mother waited that evening for news of Damin.

Majang came at sundown, rejoicing to find them so cozy in their new quarters. He told them that Damin would stay at the hospital for two or three days, because the doctor wanted to watch the sickness for a little while.

"He is just the same." Majang sighed. "He cares for nothing and sits on his mat there at the hospital just as he does here."

"Do you think he will feel lonely?" Teejah was busy arranging the pots and kettles in the new kitchen.

"The Tuan will go to see him every day." Majang stepped to the rice bin and lifted the lid. It was a fine, large rice bin, newly built. "Not much is left." Majang let the lid fall.

"There is enough to last us for quite a while," Teejah hastened to reassure him. She went to the wooden chest and brought out the roll of money from the orchid. "How wonderful that we have this money. I think it will be enough to furnish us with rice until the harvest."

9. Strong Medicine

MEN FROM BULUNO VILLAGE came every day to work on the house. They were not always the same ones, but they were always men who listened to the teacher, Rindoo. Every day these men left their own work and came to help with the building of Teejah's new home. This new house was not made like the other houses in the village. It had a large veranda, facing the village and the mountain. Few of the people of Lansat Village had ever seen such a thing before, and even Teejah wondered about the reason for it.

Finally the day came when the Tuan and Rindoo brought Damin back from the hospital. They fetched him into the new house, for Teejah and Pala had already moved in. They sat him down on a mat. There was no change in his condition, and Teejah looked at her son with a heaviness of heart it was not possible to conceal.

"Call Pala." The Tuan sat down on the mat beside Damin. "Majang is down the road. He will soon be here."

Teejah sensed that this was a solemn moment. She drew Pala close, and when Majang came in they all sat down like people in a council.

"The doctor at the hospital says that the long fever burned away something in Damin's head," Rindoo told them. "He says there is nothing he can do for him." Rindoo spoke with great earnestness. "But we who believe in the God of Heaven know that when men can do nothing, then they must put their trust in Him. I am going home now to Buluno Village. I will call all the believers together and we will fast and pray to the God of Heaven and ask him to bring back the lost mind of Damin."

Then the Tuan spoke to Teejah and Pala. Though he could not speak their language well, they knew that he was trying to give them comfort and hope. They knew that kindness and friendliness were round about them and they did not feel alone.

When the visitors rose to go, Teejah bade them "Peaceful journey" without tears, and turned back to the pleasant duty of preparing supper for the boys.

In spite of Teepoo's curse, some of the village women began to come to see the new house. They asked endless questions about who built it, how much it cost, and the reason for the large veranda.

"Teepoo says that Damin will always be as he is now," one of the women informed Teejah. "He is cursed because of this new witchcraft."

"Teepoo says that the fever left the boys because of the medicine he made. If you had waited one day before calling the white Tuan, you would have seen for yourself," said another.

"But I couldn't wait. Don't you remember that Teepoo said the devil had gone into Pala's front teeth and they must be knocked out at once? That is why I sent for the white Tuan. He has skill to pull teeth," Teejah tried to explain to them. "Besides, the medicine of the black book is good." She became bolder and more positive as she talked. "It gives me peace here." She laid her hand over her heart. "I know that Damin's mind was destroyed because of the long fever. If I had called Rindoo sooner, it might not be so. Majang advised me to call Rindoo, but my heart was blind then. I had faith in Teepoo and I refused."

"Do you know that Teepoo is making strong devil medicine against this house? He has buried the charms," the first woman said, with a finality that seemed to pronounce certain doom for the new house.

"You should not stay here, not even for another night," the second visitor advised.

"It is very dangerous," the third urged. "You had better come home with me to my house."

Teejah answered with patience. "I have heard words from the black book saying that even the hairs of our heads are all counted by the God of Heaven. This shows that he loves us with a great love. I am no longer afraid of the curses and charms of devils. I thank you for your kindness, but I will stay in my house and pray to the God of Heaven."

Teejah stood on her veranda and watched the women go back to their own homes, chattering like a flock of ricebirds as they went. So Teepoo had already buried devil charms beside this new house. He must have come in the night and buried them, for the workers still came every day to work on the fence around the big veranda. It would be impossible to discover where the little bundle of bones and hair and sticks was concealed. In the former days, belief that such charms were working against her would have filled Teejah with frenzied apprehension. But now peace filled her heart. She knew that the God of Heaven had taken her under his protection.

"Mother," Pala asked one evening, "do you think Damin will get well when Rindoo and the people of Buluno make the medicine of the God of Heaven?"

This question had been forming itself in Teejah's own heart, and in the strength of her new faith she replied, "Yes, Pala, I believe it. And I too will pray to the God of Heaven that Damin may be restored."

The following day two men from Buluno came and finished clearing up all the rubbish from the old hut. Everything was done now. The new house was complete. Then for two days no one came.

The next evening Teejah was busy preparing supper. She piled a plate with rice and set it before Pala, who was always hungry these days. Then, as her custom was, she went to bring Damin from the inner room so that he might sit with his brother and eat his rice.

Teejah's heart stood still for an instant, then began to pound like a padi pounder. Damin was not on his mat. He was standing at the window looking at the brilliant sunset. Teejah clung to the doorjamb to steady herself.

Damin heard her step and turned to look at her with puzzled eyes. "Mother, what house is this? I see the spring and the rice field. What house is this?"

Teejah cried out with joy and threw herself into

her son's arms, weeping and trembling all over from the gladness that filled her heart. Pala, hearing his mother's cry, came to the doorway and stood staring in astonishment at his brother.

"Tell me, Pala, what house is this?" Damin asked. "Have I been asleep? I remember that the day before yesterday Majang and I came back from Togop."

"Oh, Damin, you have been sick for many days. You had the fever." Pala was so excited that he could scarcely talk. As for Teejah, she could only cling to Damin and weep for joy.

"Come, little Mother, I am hungry." Damin drew her out into the kitchen room of the new house. "Let us eat the rice and you two can tell me all about it." Damin realized that something extraordinary must have happened and it would take a little time to understand it all. The boys ate a hearty supper, but Teejah could eat nothing because of the fullness of joy and thankfulness that overflowed her heart.

There was much to tell and the excitement was

so great that Damin stopped eating every little while and looked from one to the other of the two dear faces, trying to grasp everything. He did understand at last that the old hut had been torn down and that the people of Buluno Village who believed in the God of Heaven had built this new house.

"We must go at once to Buluno Village," Teejah said to the boys when they had finished eating. "We must tell Rindoo and the believers there that Damin is well—he has been brought back again."

She explained to Damin that during his terrible sickness the medicine of Teepoo had been tried. She had given all the possessions of the family to Teepoo in payment for that medicine, but no healing had come of it. Then she had asked the young teacher, Rindoo, to come and he had sent for the white Tuan.

Damin listened in great wonder. "The God of Heaven has brought me back," he said at last with reverence and delight.

After preparing resinous flares, the three of

them set off for Buluno Village, talking as they went.

"Teepoo laid a curse on our house and on you," Pala blurted out. "He said you would always be an idiot."

"The God of Heaven is stronger than all the curses of Teepoo," Teejah answered.

On reaching Buluno Village they went to Majang's house, but he was not there. Curious villagers asked them their errand and directed them to Rindoo's home. The door was closed, but through the cracks in the *kajang* they could see that a light burned inside and they could hear the sound of talking. Teejah lifted her voice in a loud cry. "My brothers and sisters, open the door. Let us in. We bring you good news!"

As Rindoo threw open the door, the three visitors walked in and stood in the midst of the little group of people. "See, Damin is returned. He is himself again, even as before the sickness!" Teejah began to weep again for joy.

Rindoo took Damin's hands in both of his and

turned him so the light from the lamp fell full on his face. Then he lifted his hands and thanked the God of Heaven. Damin and Pala and Teejah were told that this was the third day since the believers in Buluno Village had begun to fast and pray for the healing of Damin.

It soon became known in the village that a wonderful thing had taken place, and many of the unbelieving villagers crowded into Rindoo's house to see the boy who had come back from the great darkness. There he stood among them, as full of life and joy as any of them.

"This is powerful medicine—powerful medicine!" they exclaimed over and over again.

It was late that night when Teejah and her sons returned again to their own house. Even after they were settled on their mats they could hardly sleep for rejoicing and wonder.

10. Roasted Padi

"I suppose Teepoo does not know," Damin said the next morning, "that his curse is broken and I am recovered of my sickness." He thought for a long time. Then he rose from his place on the mat and opened the door. "I will walk through the village and see if my baby buffalo is about. I will see what I can see. Will you come with me, Pala?"

Pala sprang to his feet and the two boys sauntered up through the village. It was still early, but they were observed and people came out of their houses as they passed. Neither boy said anything.

"It is sad to see Damin," one woman called to her neighbor. "He is nothing but a poor idiot now."

"Yes, Teepoo cursed him. He will be like that

152 MIRACLE OF THE SONG

as long as he lives." The other woman followed the boys with her sharp eyes. "It is because of the teaching from the black book," she continued in her shrill voice.

Damin and Pala walked through the village until they came to the far side where Teepoo pastured his animals. The baby buffalo was there, still following his mother, but bigger and fatter

now. Damin drew the awkward little creature to him and fondled him with affection.

"What are you doing here?" demanded Teepoo in a startled voice.

"Peaceful morning to you, Teepoo." Damin spoke respectfully. "I wanted to pet this little fellow."

Teepoo's mouth fell open in such fright and astonishment that he was unable to answer. He raised both hands to his head and stood staring.

The boys patted and scratched the baby water buffalo, waiting for Teepoo to say something, but he turned without speaking, ran into his house, and closed the door.

Damin and Pala returned as they had come, but on the way back they spoke to everyone. There were many people out among the houses, and Damin greeted them all with pleasure. Some returned the greeting, but most of them were frightened and hurried away, or scrambled into their huts and peeked out with furtive curiosity.

"Mother, the village people are all afraid of me."

Damin smiled as he entered his house. "They run as though they had seen a ghost."

"Get all the mats we have, boys," Teejah replied, laughing. "Before an hour passes most of the people in the village will come here. Their curiosity will bring them. They will have to know how this wonder came to pass."

"Look! Rindoo and Majang are coming now." Pala pointed down the path, where two figures could be seen striding along in the hot sun.

While the teacher and Majang spoke with the widow and her sons, the people began to come from all parts of the village. They came slowly, as if drawn against their will. Then, as more and more of them could be seen going to Teejah's house, the stragglers scrambled along in great haste for fear they might miss something.

It was almost noon and there was work to be done, but no one cared for that. The work could wait. The people crowded into the veranda of Teejah's house and sat down on the mats until there were no more mats; then they sat on the bare bamboo floor. Damin and his mother and brother sat among them with the teacher, Rindoo, and Majang, whose face shone with joy.

The people looked at Damin and whispered among themselves until Rindoo stood up and motioned with his hand. Then they became quiet.

"Do not be afraid, my friends." The smile on the young teacher's face reassured them all. "You can see that Damin is well again, and you are glad. You know he had the fever for many days until the thoughts of his head were burned away. You know that after his body became well his mind did not come back, and the Tuan took him to the hospital. Even there the English doctor could do nothing for him. Now you see he is entirely well. This is by the will of the God of Heaven." Rindoo drew the black book from his pocket and opened it. A murmur of excitement ran through the crowd. This was the black book from which the powerful medicine was made. They had all heard about it.

"This is the Word of the God of Heaven." Rindoo held the book high so they could all see it. "Call upon me in the day of trouble. I will deliver thee and thou shalt glorify me." Rindoo read these words in a loud voice. Then he explained that the love of God for his people is greater than the love a father has for his children. He told them that everyone can pray to the God of Heaven and find him full of kindness.

There was much that Damin did not understand. There was even more that the village people could not understand, for they had never heard such things before. But everyone did realize that peace and great happiness filled the house of the widow and her two sons, and that thanks for the marvelous thing that had happened were being given to the God of Heaven. This was all they could take in at one time.

Rindoo did not speak long. "This place has been prepared," Rindoo said, "in order that you may come here to listen to the words of the God of Heaven and learn to sing his praises. You may come every night. Do not be afraid."

Then at last Teejah understood why the large veranda had been built on the new house, and her heart was filled with joy.

"We must begin early to prepare our rice field," Teejah told the boys a few days later. "We will have to do all the plowing with the heavy grub hoe, and it will take a long time."

The boys had just eaten a good breakfast and were feeling full of energy. "Are we going to clear new land this year?" Damin was thoroughly interested.

"Yes, I think we should. I think we should clear a spot back in the swamp yonder, beyond the old tree. It is good fat soil."

So the two boys and their mother, armed with curved jungle knives, went out that day to the swampy land near the spring. As they passed the big old tree, they marked with sadness that the rains had washed a deep hole where the roots had been cut that day when Teepoo was so sure the devils were hiding in the tree.

"We must fill up that hole," Damin said. "Why are all the roots on this side cut away?"

"Teepoo said the devil was hiding in the tree and making you sick, so we cut it to frighten the devils away." Teejah looked down at the hole. "I think we should not fill it up yet. I am afraid the tree will die. We may have to cut it down."

They worked all morning cutting down the thick undergrowth, and then they lunched briefly in the shade of the old tree. Teejah had prepared rice cakes boiled in coconut milk. Each rice cake was wrapped in a banana leaf and this gave a pleasant flavor to the cooked rice.

"I have asked Majang to buy us five hens," Teejah told the boys that evening. "Perhaps they will lay us some eggs and we can raise some baby chicks and have a flock of chickens again."

When Majang came with the hens, both boys were surprised and excited. They were not like any hens they had seen before. They were larger than ordinary ones and their color was a beautiful red.

"What kind of chickens are those?" Teejah demanded of Majang as he untied the legs of the five hens and turned them loose in the old chicken yard.

"I don't know," he confessed. "They are from

the Tuan's place. I think they come from China, or America, or some other foreign country."

"Mother, may I have the hen with the black feather in her tail?" Pala pointed out the one he wanted.

"Certainly you may have her." Teejah laughed with pleasure at Pala's eagerness.

"She can take the place of my black cock." Pala was over the fence in a flash and caught the red hen in his arms, burying his face in her soft feathers.

The days went by filled with hard work for the widow's family as they prepared the new rice field, but in the evenings the gatherings on the veranda of the little house gave them joy. At first many people of Lansat Village came to listen and to sing. Some came only from curiosity, and after a few evenings they did not come back. But there were several families who came every night, and it was evident that the teachings of the black book had taken hold of them.

"Teepoo is angry at this new teaching," Damin told Pala as they worked at preparing the seed bed for the new rice field. "He has said that he will drive this magic of the black book from Lansat Village."

"I wonder what he will do." Pala slithered his hands about in the soft mud of the seed bed. "What can he do, Damin?"

"I think he may try in some way to make his curses come true," Damin answered gravely. "He was very cruel. He can be cruel again."

"Then we must be watchful," Pala said with a solemn face.

The seed bed was ready to plant, but they had no good seed rice. Teejah always saved the best of her harvest for future planting, but this year the seed rice had been taken from her or used during the boys' sickness. So it was with glad surprise that the family welcomed a woman who came that morning with a gift of rice.

"Teejah," said the visitor, "we know that you have no seed rice and we see that your seed bed is

ROASTED PADI

ready to plant. Teepoo is sorry for you, so he has sent you this seed rice. He hopes your crops will be good." She set down a woven grass bag of padi and hurried away.

Teejah turned to the boys. "See, even Teepoo is growing kind," she said with delight.

Damin made no reply. He shouldered the bag of padi and carried it out to the seed bed, where he set it down. "Pala!" He spoke in a low strained voice. "I am sure there is something wrong with this padi. Teepoo would not have given it to us otherwise."

"But it looks all right, Damin." Pala had opened the bag and was sifting the kernels of padi through his fingers.

The boys went to the house to eat. When they returned to the seed bed, Damin took a mat with him. He dumped the seed padi on the mat and knelt beside it to investigate it thoroughly. "Look, Pala!" he cried. "This padi has been roasted! It will never grow!" He held out his hand and showed his brother three or four kernels that looked as if they had been burned. "It was a clever job, too, but not clever enough." Damin's face was hot. He hardly knew whether it was from excitement or anger.

"We will not tell our mother of this," Damin admonished Pala. "Not yet. I have a plan." Pala listened eagerly as he and Damin gathered up the mat and poured the padi back into the sack. "Majang told me that the government has seed padi that they will give to the village people. Some of it is red. Some is white. Some has long grains. Some of the grains are almost round. Then some of it is sticky rice, the *pooloot* Mother uses to make cakes. We must go to Majang and ask him for some of this seed rice."

"Why don't all the village people ask for it if the government will give it?" Pala was puzzled.

"Majang says a small bag of each kind is given and each one must be planted by itself. Our people do not wish to make separate plantings."

"That would be a lot of work." Pala stretched and gave a sigh. "Mother will expect us to plant this seed from Teepoo," he said in a troubled voice. "What shall we tell her?"

Damin considered this question for just a minute. "It won't hurt to plant it." He laughed. "It will fertilize the seed bed. But not one kernel of it will grow. Teepoo has made sure of that."

So the two boys sowed the roasted padi thick in the soft mud of the seed bed. Then they asked their mother if they might go to Majang's house. It was already afternoon, but she gave them permission and they started for Buluno Village at a brisk trot.

Majang was working in his own rice field. He looked up at the boys with a welcoming smile and asked them the reason for their coming.

"Rindoo said that the government will give rice for planting," Damin began. "We would like to try some of it."

Majang went into his hut and came out with three small bags of padi. "There are six kinds. The Tuan thought you might like to try them and I was planning to bring them over in the morning."

"Why does the government give the seed padi?" Pala was still curious.

"The Tuan says that the government people wish the villagers to have good rice crops. They think some of these new kinds of seed may give more and better rice than the old kind." The boys followed Majang into the hut, where he collected three more bags of padi and put them in Damin's arms.

"Every boat that comes in brings rice. The people of this country do not raise enough rice to feed those who live here. Some of the rice comes from China, some from Siam. If we had the right kind of rice and knew how to plant and harvest it properly, we could raise enough rice for everyone." Majang seemed to know a lot about the matter.

Damin considered this. "The government is good." He gave Pala three of the small sacks of padi and tied the other three in his scarf. "We are grateful to the government and to the Tuan."

As the boys walked home they talked together

about how they could plant the seed bed without letting their mother know about the new seed. "She will think it is strange when she finds we have cut the seed bed into six parts." Pala shifted the weight of his load of padi. "And Majang is sure to say something about it."

"I think we shall have to tell her." Damin had already made this decision. "I am sure this is not the last scheme Teepoo will try in order to do us harm. She had better be watchful too."

So when the boys got home they carried the bags of seed padi directly to their mother and told her the whole story of how they had discovered Teepoo's deception. They told also of the kindness of the government and the Tuan, who had thought of them and sent out the rice for them to plant.

Teejah's eyes darkened with something deeper than anger as she listened to the boys' talk. Without saying a word, she rose from the mat where she had been sitting weaving a basket, and went to the clay stove. She picked up a pot of curry. Both boys smelled the delicious curry and were eager to begin eating. "A woman from the village brought this curry while you were away. She was not the woman who brought the seed padi, but I suspect now that the curry may have come from the same place." Teejah had the same look of darkness in her eyes. "You boys must not taste it and neither will I." She returned the pot to the stove.

"But, Mother, what could be wrong with the curry?" Pala was hungry.

"Perhaps nothing is wrong, Pala. I was grateful for it until just now." Teejah looked at him, tenderness creeping back into her eyes. "But those who would give us roasted padi to plant in the seed bed might also offer a gift of food that had better not be eaten. Look, here is boiled fish and greens. You may eat this with your rice." She ladled out full plates for them both.

While the boys ate, Teejah brought a basin close to the coconut-oil lamp, for night had fallen. Into it she poured some water from the bamboo container and a little of the gravy from the curry. She mixed it well and shook it around, peering all the while into the basin. The boys watched, fascinated. Finally she scooped up in her hand the portion that floated on the surface of the water and held it out in the faint light for both boys to see. On her hand lay many small dark slivers that looked like short hairs.

"What is it, Mother?" Both boys stopped eating and looked at her hand.

"Take a length of green bamboo tomorrow and shave the fine prickles from it. You will find they are the same as this."

"But what harm can they do?" Damin still did not understand.

"These fine hairs are so small and so soft that no one can notice them when they are eaten in curry or vegetables. But they are sharp, and when they get into the stomach they stick fast all through one's body and cause a great soreness and sickness, for which there is no cure. This is not an uncommon thing. I have heard of it often before, but never in this village."

"May I see what you have found in the curry?" A sudden voice from the door startled them all. They looked up to see Majang standing there with

two small paper bags in his hand. "I heard what you said, Teejah." Majang's face was black with anger. "I am sure the headmen and the chief of Lansat Village have no knowledge of this wickedness of Teepoo's. It is time for me to inform them." Majang started out the door, then remembered the paper bags. "I tried to overtake the boys, but they went too fast. This is some fertilizer the Tuan said to mix with the mud in the seed bed. I forgot to give it to them when they got the rice. I knew

they would be planting early in the morning, so I came now."

After Majang had gone, Damin went outside the house and walked alone in the dark night. His mind was whirling with thoughts that had never been there before. So this was the way of darkness in the heart of a wicked man. A devouring rage consumed him as he thought of all his mother had suffered at the hands of the witch doctor. Then he reflected on the protection that had been granted them. It had all come about in a simple, natural way, but the warnings were there. Suppose they had not agreed to tell their mother about the roasted seed rice! Would they have eaten the curry for supper? Probably.

The words of the song flashed into Damin's mind: "God will take care of you." He did not feel like singing, but the words suddenly held for him the ring of vital truth. Peace flooded back into his heart, and with it a great pity for one who could do such wrong.

Majang did not come back that night, and it

was not until the next day that Teejah and the boys heard of Teepoo's departure from Lansat Village. The village women brought the news early in the morning.

"Teepoo has gone, Teejah," one of them said.

"Last night Majang told the chief and the headmen about the bamboo hairs in your curry," said another.

"The chief was angry and he went to Teepoo's house and asked him about it." A third woman supplied her part of the story. "Teepoo became so angry that we all knew it was he who had done it. He acted like a madman."

"The chief told him to leave," the first woman said. "He was not willing to go, but the headmen threatened to inform the government officer if Teepoo did not leave Lansat Village. The chief said he will inform the government at once if Teepoo ever shows his face here again."

Teejah sat for a moment with her head bowed. Poor old Teepoo! He had lived all his life in Lansat Village, and he had been more powerful than the chief in days gone by. "I hope Teepoo will think over all the things that have happened and see that there is great power in the medicine of the black book. It is useless for him to fight against that medicine and the God of Heaven."

Damin said nothing, but the wave of relief and thankfulness that swept over him lifted his heart still closer to the God of Heaven, who counts even the hairs of his children's heads.

11. Some Surprises

NONE OF THE WIDOW'S FAMILY were prepared for the surprise that came later that morning. Shouting was heard outside the house and the boys hurried out to see who had come. It was Majang. He was leading the baby water buffalo, grown bigger now, but still fat and full of tricks. Both boys embraced the shaggy little creature with rough affection.

"But how did you get him?" they both asked.

Teejah came out of the house with a troubled look on her face. "Did Teepoo send Damin's baby buffalo back to us?" she asked with apprehension in her voice.

"Oh, no, not he!" Majang laughed and slapped his knee as he always did when much pleased.

"Teepoo is gone! Haven't you heard? He was driven out of Lansat Village last night. His wickedness is known to all, and he will never return or try any more of his evil tricks on any of us. The day before he left he sold the baby buffalo to the Chinese butcher, and Rindoo bought him."

"But why? What for? Where did he get the money? Such a young buffalo would bring at least ten dollars at the market." Teejah was much agitated.

"Yes, that is what Rindoo paid for him. You see, Teepoo took the buffalo to the market, and Rindoo saw him and asked the Chinese butcher to buy the little fellow for him."

Majang laughed again. He thought it was a wonderful joke.

"But Rindoo is poor. How could he afford to buy the baby water buffalo for Damin?" Teejah was still troubled.

"He gets a few dollars a month," Majang assured her. "He has been saving ever since he heard about Teepoo's taking away Damin's pet." Majang stood patting the little water buffalo. "You must not refuse to accept his gift, Teejah. He would be hurt in the heart. He is as happy as Damin."

The surprise of the baby buffalo was still delighting the two boys as they ate breakfast the next morning, but another surprise was in store. Majang appeared with Rindoo and all the other men who had worked to build the new house.

"We have come to prepare your rice field." Rindoo was dressed in old clothes like the others, so that Teejah and the boys scarcely recognized him. He was carrying a heavy grub hoe like the rest and was evidently planning to work with them.

Before Teejah and Damin could ask any questions, the men had gone to the rice field and started to work. The widow and her sons followed with their own implements, and together they all worked in the field. It was amazing what so many people could do in so short a time. The mud flew, and skillful hands built the small mud walls that would mark the divisions between the sections of the rice field. Bamboo drains were placed in these mud dikes so the flow of water from one section of the field to another could be controlled. The men had brought food with them and paused briefly to eat. Then they worked until the sun was going down.

"I think one more day will finish it." Majang was weary, but much pleased over what had been accomplished. "We shall return tomorrow."

SOME SURPRISES 177

Within the next few weeks sturdy green sprouts began to show in the seed bed. "It must be that roasted padi is the best kind of fertilizer." Damin laughed and knelt to feel the stems. "We never had better plants than these." He pulled one up and handed it to his mother for inspection.

During the following days Teejah's rice field was set with the plants from the six sections of the seed bed. Rain fell every day and constant care

was needed to see that the water in each division of the field stayed at exactly the right depth. Day and night Teejah and the boys watched over the new plants until they could see from the fresh, springing green that the roots had taken hold in the rich mud. Even then they still gave a good deal of attention to the field. Each one of the six sections was going to be different. Each would be a surprise. It was hard to wait. The plants, which had been little larger than a single blade of grass when they were set out, now filled out and multiplied. The waving green was a glorious color.

The days were full of work and the evenings were pleasant with song. The new teaching from the black book drew those who accepted it close together. Friends became dearer. Even in Lansat Village there were people who were close to Teejah now.

At last the time for the rice harvest drew near. In every one of the six sections of their field, the widow and her sons could see the heavy heads of a bountiful harvest. Some varieties of the rice were tall and some were short, but all were healthy and abundant. Teejah and Damin could hardly wait for the time of reaping.

Then the day came when the two boys and their mother, with woven rice baskets strapped to their chests, went into the field to cut the ripened crop. Each day they cut one of the six sections and carried the heavy heads of rice into the veranda, where they had spread out tightly woven mats. Each day they eagerly trod out the rice and sacked it, marking the different varieties as the small bags of seed had been marked. At the end of the sixth day it was all gathered in, and Damin and his mother knew that there had never been so heavy a crop of rice on so small a field in their village.

"It is the blessing of the God of Heaven," Teejah exclaimed to Majang and Rindoo, when they came to admire the full rice bin, partitioned now into six compartments. "What can we do to show our gratitude?"

"Give to the God of Heaven one tenth of all your harvest." Rindoo answered the question without hesitation.

"Help me to separate it now," Teejah urged the

men. "I will hull the rice for the God of Heaven and sell it in the market."

"No, Teejah, I do not think you should hull this padi, and I do not think you should take it to market. This rice of yours is exceptionally fine and will be in great demand as seed rice. The government has not enough seed for all who ask for it. It will be good for the village if you share your fine harvest with them."

"Should I give it to them?" Teejah was anxious to do everything just right.

"Not unless they are too poor to pay for it. We usually exchange one measure of seed rice for two measures of ordinary padi. If you want to be really kind to your neighbors, you could exchange measure for measure. Then you can hull the rice you receive, sell it at the market, and pay your tithe that way."

It turned out just as Rindoo had said. Teejah's padi was in great demand. Everyone in the village wanted some to plant. All Teejah's tithe rice was soon exchanged for the ordinary kind and the grateful villagers rejoiced over their good fortune.

Now that the harvest was over, Damin began to make other plans. "I wish we could have a church and a school in this village," he said to his mother. "I am going to talk to Rindoo about it. I know that all the believers here will be glad to make such a building. We can still use the veranda for singing."

But when Damin talked with Rindoo, the young teacher thought they would have to wait for another year. The materials for the building would cost too much for the people to buy right now. But in spite of what Rindoo said, Damin could not get the idea out of his mind. He thought about it while he gathered materials for building a fence, and while he strengthened the few weak spots in the *kajang* walls and *attap* roof of the new house.

The rains grew more violent. A sudden storm came one night with strong winds and floods of rain. Early in the morning Damin was awakened by a crash. The old *buluno* tree had gone down! With its weakened roots it could not stand against the storm.

At dawn Damin went out to look at it. The top of the big old tree lay near the house, and there among the thick leaves of the highest branches he saw an orchid plant! So great was his delight and excitement that he hacked furiously with his belt knife until he had loosened the plant with all its roots. It was large and filled with swelling buds. He carried it in to his mother.

"Oh, Mother," he cried. "See what I found in

the top of our big old tree!" Damin danced about the room with the heavy plant in his hands. Teejah had to laugh at him.

"This is different from the mountain orchids," he said. "It will soon bloom. See how big the buds are!"

Teejah took the precious plant and hung it below the window on the sunny side of the house.

Every evening the people gathered to sing. Even in the rainy time they came, and the peace of the village was great. There were some who did not believe, but these were treated so kindly by the Christian believers that one by one they came to worship with the rest. The backbone of heathen witchcraft was broken forever in the village of Lansat. More and more Damin took over the leadership of the village worship. It was evident to everyone that the God of Heaven had laid a special charge on him.

It was only a few days after the storm that had brought down the old tree when the orchid opened its first blossom. It was a white flower with a yellow throat!

"Mother!" Damin clasped his hands in reverent wonder as he looked at the marvelous beauty of the flower. "To think that it was right here in Lansat Village all the time and I didn't know it!" Damin touched the leaves with loving fingers. "I will wait until the flowers are in full bloom and then I will carry it to the white Tuan in Jesselton."

Majang came to look at the orchid a few days later. "I think this plant is ready to carry to Jesselton." He looked the white orchid over with critical eyes. "I will go with you tomorrow if you wish."

The next day the two of them, almost hidden by the large plant with its dazzling flowers, stood at the door of the government official who had requested that all white orchids be brought to him. It was still early, for Damin and Majang had started from Lansat Village before sunrise.

"What a beauty! What a beauty!" the delighted Tuan exclaimed, and he called his wife to see the lovely sight. "It is the finest one I have ever seen," he said. Then he led Damin and Majang to the back garden of his house and opened the gate.

They went through and saw a sight that they could scarcely believe, even though they saw it in the bright light of day.

Between two trees was a wide ladder made of thick logs. Each log was about twelve feet long and they extended up and back like a stairway for fifteen feet. On these logs were fastened orchid plants like the one in Damin's hands. All of them were in full bloom, and they made a waterfall of white blossoms with golden throats. Neither Damin nor Majang could say anything. They looked and gasped. Surely no sight so beautiful had ever been seen before.

Then the Tuan took the plant from Damin. "This is the queen of them all. I will fasten it at the top in the place of highest honor." Damin still stood speechless. "What are you going to do with the money I shall give you?" the white man asked.

"I will use it to help build a church in our village." Damin looked the Tuan straight in the eye.

"Then make it twice as much," the Tuan called to his wife. She came out with a roll of paper money, which she gave to Damin.

Damin never did tell how much the reward was, but it was enough to buy at once all the materials for the new church, with a schoolroom behind it. Damin insisted that it should stand beside the spring where the great tree had once stood. Most of the men in the village worked at building it, and before many days the church was finished.

The heart of Damin sang for joy as he stood with Rindoo in the fine new house of worship for the God of Heaven.

"Now the God of Heaven has his home in our village." Damin smiled at his teacher. "We shall all learn more about his love for us."

"What is the sure way by which the God of Heaven shows us his care and kindness?" Rindoo asked the boy.

Damin was quick with the answer. "By filling the hearts of men and women with loving-kindness. Are we not all one in God?"

We invite you to view the complete
selection of titles we publish at:

www.TEACHServices.com

Scan with your mobile
device to go directly
to our website.

Please write or e-mail us your praises, reactions, or
thoughts about this or any other book we publish at:

P.O. Box 954
Ringgold, GA 30736

info@TEACHServices.com

TEACH Services, Inc., titles may be purchased in bulk for
educational, business, fund-raising, or sales promotional use.
For information, please e-mail:

BulkSales@TEACHServices.com

Finally, if you are interested in seeing
your own book in print, please contact us at

publishing@TEACHServices.com

We would be happy to review your manuscript for free.

www.ingramcontent.com/pod-product-compliance
Lightning Source LLC
Chambersburg PA
CBHW070537170426
43200CB00011B/2455